LEARNING TO DRIVE IN PICTURES

BY
A. TOM TOPPER

PAPERFRONTS
ELLIOT RIGHT WAY BOOKS
KINGSWOOD, SURREY, U.K.

Made and printed in Great Britain by
C. Nicholls & Company Ltd.
and published by
Elliot Right Way Books
Kingswood, Surrey, U.K.

Contents

GENERAL GUIDANCE   13

PART ONE
LEARNING TO HANDLE THE CAR

HOW TO SIT   17
Holding the wheel. Adjusting the seat. Secure the seat. How to adjust the mirrors.

LEARNING TO USE THE CONTROLS BY TOUCH AND FEEL   19
The foot pedals and how they control the car. The accelerator and its job. Pulling power. The gears. The clutch. How the clutch works. The gear lever. Holding the gear lever. The footbrake explained. The handbrake explained.

OPEN SPACE PRACTICE   26
Jerky starts. Find an open space. The theory of steering. Hand movements. The smooth start from standing. Using the choke. Keep both hands on the wheel. Learning to stop. Braking at slow speeds. The feet positions. Braking at faster speeds. Emergency stops. Mile-an-hour driving. Gear speeds. How to change the gears. Early open space targets. More helpful open space training exercises. Reversing. Stopping in reverse. The eyes when reversing. Steering in reverse.

CAR CONTROL TESTS ON "TEST"   46
The three point turn. Stop properly at kerb. Road camber. The turn itself. The reverse into a side-road opening. The uphill start. Downhill starts. Hill parking.

PART TWO
GENERAL ROAD AND TRAFFIC DRIVING

BEGINNING ON THE ROAD   56
Get experience. Study all of the book before driving. Checking the doors. A running commentary. Concentration. Notes for teachers. Mirrors. More about stopping in an emergency. Emergency stop "on test".

VARIOUS ROAD SITUATIONS   61
Moving off. Ordinary two way roads. How fast should I go?
Road narrows. A golden rule. Country lanes. Hooting. Hairpin
bends. Turning into a steep opening. Dual carriageways.

FOLLOWING OTHERS   66
Thinking time. The gap to leave. Leaving room for others to
overtake. Braking from speed. Seeing beyond the car in front.
Warning people behind. The gears in traffic. The gears for going
uphill. Rain and wet.

READING THE ROAD   70
Training your eyes. Two "experts'" tips. More refined road
reading.

PEDESTRIAN CROSSINGS   73
Right of way. Gradualness the secret. Stop! Children Crossing
patrols.

GIVING WAY AND YOUR "SUPPOSED" RIGHTS   74
If being overtaken. Obstructions. Passing parked cars. Passing
cyclists. Meat in a sandwich. Lane discipline. Narrow "hump-
back" bridges.

OVERTAKING   79
The secret. Get back to safety. The warning hoot. Three
"overtaking" questions. Overtaking on three lane – two way –
roads. Avoid the sandwich pass. Room for me too?

PART THREE
TACKLING THE MANY KINDS OF ROAD JUNCTION

TURNING LEFT   85
Whose right of way? Turning left off a major road at a T
junction. Left turn at a stop sign onto a major road. Looking right
and left. Left turn at a give way sign onto a major road. Positioning
for left turns. Positioning leaving a minor road to go left. Positioning leaving a major road. Turning left at crossroads onto a major
road. Left turns off the major road at crossroads. Don't overtake
others who are turning left.

TURNING RIGHT   92
Procedure leaving a minor road. Positioning to turn right onto
a major road. At the turn when the law says stop. At the turn

when the law says give way. A positional "catch" turning right onto a major road. Method for right turns off a major road. Hidden dangers turning right. Right turns at crossroads. Turning right from the minor road at crossroads. Turning right off a major road at crossroads.

GOING STRAIGHT AHEAD   99
When on a major road. At crossroads if you are on the minor road. A quick glance and away is not good enough. Which queue?

UNMARKED CROSSROADS   101
Beware. Watch out for other people. Headlight flashing.

SIGNALS   102
When and how to signal. Flashers "system". Hand signals. Right hand signal. Slowing down signal. Left hand signal. Signals to police.

HAND SIGNALS "SYSTEM"   104
Timing right and left hand signals arriving at a major road. Timing right and left hand signals leaving a major road. The slow down signal. Signals when going straight on at crossroads.

MORE DIFFICULT TURNING AND SIGNAL PROBLEMS   106
When a late signal is correct. Another need for a late signal. A vital tip. Positioning. Turning left and, almost immediately, right. Turning right and, almost immediately, left. Introducing a golden rule.

DUAL CARRIAGEWAY TURNS   110
The safe area for turners. Turning right onto a dual carriageway. Right turns off a dual carriageway. Left turns at dual carriageways. Don't make a mistake.

TRAFFIC LIGHTS   112
Light sequences. The chief dangers at lights. Approaching lights. Waiting at lights. Danger from pedestrians if turning. Pedestrian "Cross" signs. Arrows on the road at lights. Signs at lights. Green filter arrows. A problem turning right. If red reappears before you get clear. Crossing in front when turning right. The light shooter. The two wheel queue jumper.

POLICEMEN ON POINT DUTY.   121
Policemen. Traffic wardens.

ONE WAYS   122
    Merging. More difficult merging. An L driver's nightmare?

ROUNDABOUTS   124
    Approaching roundabouts. Signals at roundabouts. Left at the
first exit. Other exits. Once on the roundabout. Spotlight on
difficulties. "Round the Block", roundabouts.

MULTIPLE CROSSROADS   129
    Attitudes. Examples of danger.

PART FOUR
SPECIAL SITUATIONS YOU MAY MEET – QUESTIONS – THE TEST

WEATHER   132
    Fog. Fog in patches. Cloudbursts, torrential rain. Spitting rain.

NIGHT DRIVING   134
    Twilight or poor light. Headlight driving. The headlight
dipswitch. Which beam? Speed. Dazzling. In the country. In
the town. More in the country. Reversing at night.

AUTOMATIC TRANSMISSION   137
    Only the right foot. The selector lever. Kickdown. General
hints and some pitfalls. Wet or greasy roads. A new automatic.

SOME SIGNS   141
    More signs. Herring bone lines. Double white lines. Road
works.

FRIGHTENING THINGS THAT CAN HAPPEN AS YOU
DRIVE   144
    Burst tyres and punctures. Accelerator sticks full on. Running
out of petrol. Windscreen shatters. Engine stalls. (stops). Brake
failure. Breakdowns on fast roads.

SKIDS   148
    Can skids be controlled? The nature of skids. Locked brakes.
Skids when braking hard. Prevention of skids when braking
hard. Correction of skids when braking hard. Over-acceleration
skids. Prevention of over-acceleration skids. Correction of over-
acceleration skids. Sideslip skids. Prevention of sideslip skids.
Correction of sideslip skids. General advice on skids.

FAST DRIVING 164
Speed. The AC Cobra. The limitations.

QUESTIONS AND ANSWERS 166
Questions. Answers.

MOTORWAYS AND FAST ROADS 175
Learn about them. Some tips. Mirrors on the motorway. Using the right flasher. Slowing and stopping. Drowsiness. Motorway questions. Motorway answers.

THE TEST 179
The car. You. Driving there. Announce your arrival. Before leaving home. How long is it? The examiner. Author's message.

Index 181

LIST OF PHOTOGRAPHS

(Photos are in the centre section of this book)

1. to 6. Early open space practice.

7. to 12. The three point turn in sequence

13. The "hover cover" feet position

14. Children running out.

15. Looking under vehicles.

16. Watch! Zebra crossing.

17. Where NOT to park!

18. Wandering pedestrians.

19. A blocked back window.

20. Speed limit signs.

21. to 24. Aquaplaning.

25. to 29. Parking between cars.

30. A narrow bridge.

31. Bad lane straddling.

LIST OF ILLUSTRATIONS

1.   How to sit.   17
2.   Mirror adjustment.   18
3.   How the footpedals control the car.   20
4.   Engine pulling power.   21
5.   The invisible "gate" of the gearbox.   23
6.   Holding the gear lever.   24
7.   The brake pedal.   25
8.   A typical handbrake.   26
9.   Steering hand movements.   27
10. How the rear wheels "cut" corners.   29
11. Starting from standing, first 5 moves.   32
12. Starting from standing, next 4 moves.   34
13. Clutch engagement.   35
14. Feet positioned for normal driving.   37
15. Emergency stopping.   38
16. Gear speeds.   39
17. Changing up the gears.   40
18. Changing down the gears.   41
19. Where to look when reversing.   43
20. Steering in reverse.   44
21. Danger in a car park.   45
22. Worm's eye view of a road showing the camber.   48

23.	Reverse into a limited opening from nearside.	50
24.	Reverse into a limited opening from offside.	51
25.	Hill starts.	53
26.	Using the gears going down hills.	54
27.	Parking on a hill.	55
28.	Split second mirror glances behind.	59
29.	Moving off.	61
30.	Distance from kerb in relation to speed.	62
31.	Road narrows.	63
32.	A narrow country lane.	64
33.	Flashing the eyes.	71
34.	At the ready for the horn.	72
35.	More refined eye-flashing.	73
36.	Giving way at road works.	75
37.	Passing parked cars.	76
38.	Cancel flashers after use.	77
39.	Meat in a sandwich.	77
40.	Overtaking.	80
41.	Three lane roads.	83
42.	The sandwich pass.	84
43.	Left turn off a major road at a T junction.	86
44.	"Feeding her" when crossing danger areas.	88
45.	Positioning during left turns.	90
46.	A crossroads problem.	91

47. A right turn. 93

48. A right turn off a major road. 96

49. Turning right onto a major road at a crossroads. 98

50. An unmarked crossroads. 101

51. Where a hand signal is unseen. 103

52. When a late signal is correct. 106

53. A difficult signalling problem. 106

54. Turning left and almost immediately right. 108

55. Turning right and almost immediately left. 108

56. A tip for turning left. 109

57. Dual carriageway turns. 110

58. Turns off dual carriageways. 111

59. A traffic light. 113

60. Arrows on the road. 116

61. Common signs at lights. 117

62. A green filter arrow. 117

63. A problem turning right. 118

64. Crossing in front when turning right. 120

65. A one-way street. 121

66. Difficult merging on a one-way street. 123

67. An L driver's nightmare? 124

68. A roundabout. 125

69. A difficult roundabout. 128

70. Multiple crossroads. 130

71.	The dipswitch. (floor type)	134
72.	Some signs.	141
73.	More signs.	142
74.	"Herring Bone" lines.	143
75.	Double white line with false impression.	144
76.	Common causes of stalling.	147
77.	Three types of skid.	148
78.	Skids when braking hard.	149
79.	Adverse camber.	153
80.	Over-acceleration skids.	156
81.	Sideslip skids.	159
82.	A U turn.	167
83.	A "Box" junction.	168
84.	An example of courtesy often overlooked.	174

General Guidance

This book is planned to enable you to learn to drive starting from the first time you sit in a driving seat. Follow it from picture to picture reading the accompanying explanatory text which contains hundreds of tips. My publishers have guaranteed that if you study it well you should pass your test or you can return the book for a full refund.

In part one of this book I am deliberately stressing three major principles of *beginning* to learn to drive. Notice the word *beginning* for this is the key; you cannot get into a car and drive off; first you must learn to control it, for your own safety and that of others.

The first step is to familiarise yourself with the controls – not to try to drive.

The second step is this; learn complete mastery of car control, *not* on the roads where there is *danger* and where traffic makes the task harder, but in a quiet open space. Here, you should learn to start smoothly, to stop, to steer, to emergency stop, to change gear, to reverse and so on; all these things you should know *before beginning road driving*.

Good open spaces are hard to find but worth searching for; quiet empty car parks, disused air-strips or dry fields (with farmer's permission) are examples. Failing these, choose a quiet area of side-roads (as many Motor Schools do) where there will be no danger to children. Your teacher can drive you there.

Step two is OPEN SPACE PRACTICE. Stay on this space to learn car control and do the exercises suggested.

Step three, in part one, is that once you have mastered control you learn to carry out the control exercises expected on test: The Three Point Turn: The Hill Start: The Reverse into a Side-road Opening.

Your teacher should drive to suitable quiet roads where you practise the manoeuvres until proficient. As well as giving you an awareness of traffic, the knowledge that you have attained the test standard of competence in car *control*, will do a lot to calm your nerves when you begin general road and traffic driving. No traffic situation should demand car control of a kind you have not already mastered.

These three steps should be taken in order and control *mastered* before beginning general road driving.

This is the safest way to learn.

When you remember that nearly everyone drives, just as most of us marry, you won't worry that learning may be too difficult. Rules are based on commonsense and the modern car is easy to drive. While learning you may be a passenger in the cars of experienced motorists; do ask questions that may help you.

You need a provisional licence, L plates front and back, a car which is properly taxed and insured, and an experienced driver to sit beside and guide you.

It is vital that the insurance policy is endorsed to cover you as a learner, it may cost a little extra but is essential for legal reasons.

Apply to the Driver and Vehicle Licencing Centre, Swansea, SA99 1AB (on a form from your Post Office) for your provisional licence and study any information sent with it. Test application forms are available from most post offices. Also study any information that the test centre send you with the test date.

A GOOD TEACHER

Find a teacher who has driven a long, accident-claim-free mileage. A competent teacher boosts confidence.

For most, is is wise to have a course of lessons from a driving school.

DO YOUR HOMEWORK

I will not discuss the "Highway Code" or the traffic signs in detail, however, on test, the examiner will ask you questions to see if you understand them, so you *must* study them. Study as you go and when you come to my sample questions you should know the answers. Ability to answer questions parrotwise will not ensure a test pass. Read and understand.

14

You can buy the "Highway Code" at book-sellers and stationers.

The examiner will watch your driving to see that you uphold the spirit of the code; that is, you always show consideration for other road users.

Learners who take their test in an automatic car are now restricted by their licence to automatic geared cars until they pass the test again with normal gears.

Part One

Learning To Handle
The Car

HOW TO SIT

Holding the wheel. Adjusting the seat. Secure the seat. How to adjust the mirrors.

HOLDING THE WHEEL.

Figs. 1 and 9 show you how to hold the steering wheel. Keep your thumbs on the inside surface and lightly grip around the wheel rim with the fingers.

ELBOWS AND KNEES
ABOUT HALF BENT

HEELS PIVOT ON FLOOR

Fig. 1. How to sit.

ADJUSTING THE SEAT.

With the seat properly adjusted your knees and elbows will be roughly half bent and you will find that you can depress any of the foot pedals to its *fullest extent* easily – *vital*.

With your left foot press down the extreme left pedal, (the clutch), and holding it down, move the gear lever. See that you can move it comfortably without having to lean forward.

There is an art in using the clutch and the master key is *to keep the heel of your left foot on the floor acting as a pivot.* In adjusting the seat you need to bear that in mind. Women drivers may find that high heels are helpful and short people may need a properly made backrest for the seat.

It is dangerous to sit slumped in the seat with outstretched legs. This hinders forward vision, especially near the car and can distort your impressions of distance. It also means that if you have to brake hard you may lack the strength as your leg is already too straight.

Fig. 2. Mirror adjustment. The "blind" areas shaded are *not* covered by the mirror. A car could be almost alongside you (though slightly behind) and not visible in the mirrors.

SECURE THE SEAT.

Make *certain* the seat is secure after adjustment. Were it to slide back as you braked your push would be ineffective – a possible killer.

HOW TO ADJUST THE MIRRORS.

Fig. 2 shows the mirror(s) adjusted for rearward vision. Sit normally and adjust so that you see the maximum distance the mirror covers without moving your head. On level ground it should be several hundred yards in each mirror. *The mirrors are vital – always keep them adjusted.*

LEARNING TO USE THE CONTROLS BY TOUCH AND FEEL.

The foot pedals and how they control the car. The accelerator and its job. Pulling power. The gears. The clutch. How the clutch works. The gear lever. Holding the gear lever. The footbrake explained. The handbrake explained.

With the car adjusted for you, your task is to understand the main controls. Study the next few pages, understand the controls and the theory behind them, sit in the car and practise working them, *without running the engine.*

This will be of tremendous benefit later, because muscles and reactions become experienced and get "into the groove".

Continue till you can work any control easily *without looking down.* It may take you several hourly sessions before mastering the techniques. Keep on and continually remind yourself *to look out in front.* As well as the pedals and gears, operate the important switches, lights, wipers, horn and flashing indicators, by touch or feel, as these need practice too – *learn not to look down at them.* Practise finding them quickly. Your teacher will show you how, but practise on your own.

Many motorists, now dead, would be alive if they had learned to use their eyes. If a cyclist looks down at his front wheel he soon hits something. Pain and twisted front wheels teach him to take a longer view. You can learn from the cyclist and train yourself, from the start, to keep your *eyes on the road.*

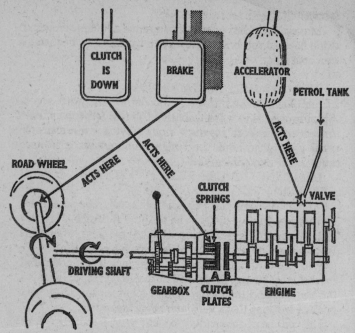

Fig. 3. How the footpedals control the car. The brake acts on all wheels

THE FOOT PEDALS AND HOW THEY CONTROL THE CAR.

These are, from your left, clutch, brake (usually similar in appearance) and accelerator. The accelerator and brake are used with the *right foot*, the clutch with the *left*.

Fig. 3 explains the use of each pedal.

For a car with automatic transmission refer to page 137 where I deal with it, but study this section and gain a working knowledge of ordinary car control.

THE ACCELERATOR AND ITS JOB.

To drive at varying speeds the engine must be fed with the right amount of petrol. The faster it goes the more petrol needed. For this purpose there is a regulating "valve" or carburettor, between the petrol tank and the engine. This is controlled by the accelerator pedal.

Pressing the pedal opens this valve to allow more petrol through, which speeds the engine. The pedal is spring loaded and returns to the lowest possible speed ("ticking over") when the foot is off the accelerator.

PULLING POWER.

Engine speeds vary from about 1,000 to 6,000 revolutions a minute. Fig. 4 shows diagrammatically how the average engine only gives its best pulling power between a limited range of R.P.M. (revolutions per minute).

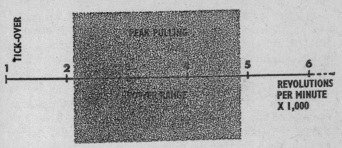

Fig. 4. Engine pulling power.

This limitation shows why it would be no use connecting the road wheels to the engine to drive the car. So that we can use maximum pulling power all the time, the speed of the engine rotation has to be geared to the speed we want the wheels to turn.

THE GEARS.

To take maximum advantage of the engine's power range, most cars have four forward gears but some have only three. 1st or bottom gear starts from standing and is used up to, on average, 10 m.p.h., a 2nd and 3rd gear are necessary for increasing speed, and a 4th or top gear is required thereafter.

You need not understand how it is done; enough to know that the gears are all together in a "gear box" as shown in fig. 3 with a lever to select which gear is wanted.

21

There is a reverse gear, operated by the same lever. This reverses the direction of rotation of the driving shaft and moves the road wheels backwards.

A neutral position, where no gear is engaged, is provided for the driver to take the car out of gear when he wishes by selecting neutral with the lever. The engine can then tick over without moving the car.

THE CLUTCH.

To change gear would be difficult without disconnecting the engine from the road wheels while the different gear cogs are meshed together.

For this we have the clutch and before using the gears you must understand it. It is designed to give a *smooth* transfer of the drive from the engine to the road wheels as you reconnect the drive by using the clutch.

HOW THE CLUTCH WORKS.

If you look at fig. 3 on page 20 you will see that the clutch consists of two circular plates facing each other. They are shown in section, separated by the clutch pedal being pressed down, so that the drive is disconnected – as if for changing gear.

The principle is simple. Plate B in fig. 3 spins with the engine at whatever speed it is running. Plate A is attached to the gear box, and, were a gear engaged, would rotate the driving shaft and the road wheels to move the car. This plate A only turns if you allow the clutch pedal to come up again, when the strong springs shown behind, force it against plate B. Once it reaches plate B and locks against it the two turn as one, taking the drive from the engine, through the gear-box, to the wheels.

Plate A approaches plate B under pressure from the springs but controlled by the clutch pedal. This pedal is your "lever" for disconnecting and re-connecting the plates.

The factor that produces a smooth engagement is the period when the two plates are only partially engaged. The period when plate A, beginning to bite against plate B already turning, starts to turn slowly itself, building up speed as it locks more tightly with plate B, until it too is turning at engine speed. The *two are then turning together without any* "slip" *being evident.*

THE GEAR LEVER.

Fig. 5 shows typical gear levers but your instructor can explain any variation in your car. The lever can only move in certain channels. They normally form an H shape with an extra arm for reverse gear. This "gate", as it is called, is

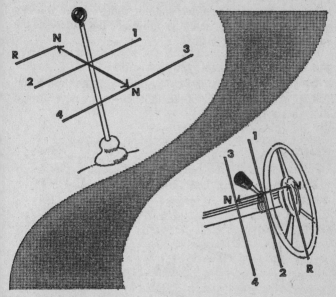

Fig. 5. The invisible "gate" of the gearbox.

concealed inside the gearbox though it can sometimes be seen in older cars. A diagram of it is often etched on the lever knob for the driver's guidance. The positions of the gears on the gate differ from car to car, so get to know the gate on your car.

The gear lever is used in conjunction with the clutch and accelerator, and you must familiarise yourself with any position quickly, *without looking down.* Practise moving the lever into the positions, (clutch pedal down).

In the N channel shown in fig. 5, the gearbox is neutralized so no gear is engaged.

The gearbox is generally made so that it is impossible to select reverse gear (R) in error. Sometimes the lever has to be "lifted" before it will slide along the neutral channel far enough to reach the reverse slot; in other cars an extra push to overcome spring loading will do, or there may be a button which has to be pressed. There are other systems but your teacher will show you.

If your car has a steering column control lever you can still imagine the gate, here it is on its side but otherwise the same. Fig. 5 also shows this.

HOLDING THE GEAR LEVER.

You do not grip it tightly but gently with the thumb and forefinger and the "ball" of the hand. Gears are never forced in, rather persuaded.

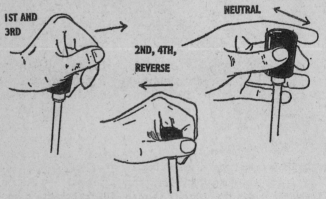

Fig. 6.   Holding the gear lever.

Fig. 6 shows the hold for 1st and 3rd (persuaded with the ball of the hand) and the slightly different hold for 2nd, top (4th) and reverse, (the hand like an eagle's claw over the lever with the pressure still taken on the ball of the hand). Checking for neutral (in which groove the lever moves freely from right to left), is also shown, using mainly the thumb and forefinger.

Practise dozens of times till you have the feel of it, and *don't look down*! Practise till you don't need to look down.

THE FOOTBRAKE EXPLAINED

See fig. 3 page 20. The footbrake acts on the wheel "disc" or the "drum" and is for stopping the car, smoothly and progressively or quickly in emergency.

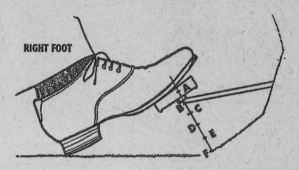

Fig. 7. The brake pedal. It should never go below approximately D when pressed.

Examine a bicycle brake and note how two pads squeeze the wheel rim, the friction created slowing the wheel. In a car the principle is similar, the backplate or disc (with disc brakes) which turns with the wheel, is braked by lined pads being squeezed against it. The pressure on the footbrake governs the degree of braking.

In fig. 7, A is the *off* position to which the spring loaded pedal automatically returns after use. Between B and D is the point where the brakes begin to act when the pedal is pressed. The action is progressive; no sudden or fierce pressure is required (emergency excepted). Gradually increasing pressure quickly stops the car. If the pedal goes to position E or F before resistance is felt, it is certain the brakes are dangerous and *need immediate repair*.

THE HANDBRAKE EXPLAINED.

This holds the car when standing. There are different types and you will need to check with your teacher how yours works. Normally a press button or a locking device is incorporated in the handle and fig. 8 shows one type. The button has to be pressed in before the handle can move to the off position.

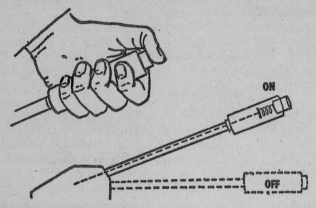

Fig. 8. A typical handbrake.

If you pull the brake on, the button normally snaps out to lock the brake on. Pressing the button in, as you pull the lever, saves wear on the ratchet. It won't hold "on" till the button is released.

Practise "off" and "on" with the handbrake while stationary, doing it by feel, not looking down. This must become instinctive which is why you need this initial, getting in "the groove", practice.

I have stressed the importance of getting to know the controls. This must be your first task. As there is no need to run the engine or drive you can practise alone. Your teacher can help with any difficulty and test you to see how quick you are. No doubt some day this practice will be done on a simulator car which Motor Schools will provide.

OPEN SPACE PRACTICE.

Jerky starts. Find an open space. The theory of steering. Hand movements. The smooth start from standing. Using the choke. Keep both hands on the wheel. Learning to stop.

Braking at slow speeds. The feet positions. Braking at faster speeds. Emergency stops. Mile-an-hour driving. Gear speeds. How to change the gears. Early open space targets. More helpful open space training exercises. Reversing. Stopping in reverse. The eyes when reversing. Steering in reverse.

JERKY STARTS.

Jerky starts are the bugbear of most learners and rank high in the "reasons for test failure" charts. For you, none of this. Follow the next few pages carefully and even the hill start will be no problem – provided you have followed the system shown.

FIND AN OPEN SPACE.

It is important to find a level open space. Search for one but if none exists use a quiet back street for early practice. But a clear space is best, even if it means your teacher has to drive some way to it.

Before moving the car study the theory of steering.

THE THEORY OF STEERING.

So far, sitting in the stationary car practising the controls – without the engine running, we have not covered steering. This was because it damages the mechanism to steer while standing unless the front wheels are jacked up. Read about steering now before putting it into practice later.

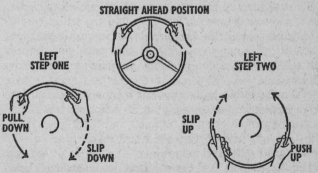

Fig. 9.   Steering hand movements.

You should be relaxed and hold the wheel gently but ready to grip in emergency. Modern steering is self centering (the mechanism tends to keep the road wheels "straight ahead"). It is bad to grip the wheel as if force were needed to keep straight. Such conscious steering results in slight weaving of the car.

Fig. 9 shows how to hold the wheel in a "quarter to three" or "ten to two" position during straight driving.

HAND MOVEMENTS.

When turning, the hands must not leave the wheel and must *never be crossed*. To turn use two basic movements repeating them alternately as needed. These are shown in fig. 9 as steps one and two. Begin with either, the important thing is the movements are repeated alternately. This method avoids crossing the hands.

Fig. 9 shows turning left. To turn right do the opposite. In step one the left hand pulls down turning the wheel; at the same time the right hand moves down allowing the wheel to slip through its fingers so that at the end of step one both hands are level, near to the bottom of the wheel, ready to start step two.

For step two the right hand pushes up and is turning the wheel while the left hand moves up again to keep level with it and ready to repeat step one.

Several movements may be necessary to put the car into full lock (the wheel as far as it will go to left or right).

To straighten up use the opposite hand movements. For *small amounts of steering* you may find the self-centering mechanism is sufficient but *you must not let go*, allowing the wheel to jerk back to straight. Rather must you control this self-centering action by lightly gripping the wheel as it slips back.

Normally, little wheel movement is enough, especially at higher speeds. Later, on the road, it is only in turning at junctions, cornering acutely, reversing and "tight" manoeuvring that you have to turn the wheel much. Practice will show you how the car responds.

The steering acts on the front wheels, so immediately you turn the wheel (with the car moving), the front starts to turn. The back wheels and the rest of the car follow. The back wheels describe a smaller circle than the front wheels which have to swing round a wider circle. You will understand this best by looking at fig. 10.

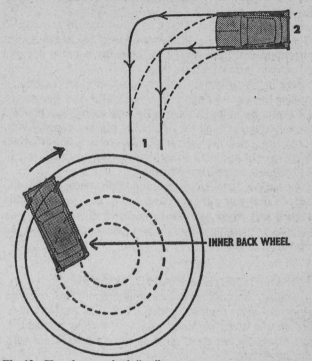

Fig. 10. How the rear wheels "cut" corners.

In fig. 10, note that if the lock could be made tight enough the car would pivot on the inner back wheel (arrowed), without that wheel moving from one spot! (This is an imaginary condition and assumes that the front wheels are driving wheels – they would have to be at right angles to the car.)

Fig. 10 also shows how the back of the car, in following round, "cuts" the corner. The heavy lines mark the path of the steering wheels, the dotted ones, the path of the rear ones.

On the road, this effect is normally only important if a sharp turn is taken too close to the kerb, as the back wheels would mount it. Don't worry over this, as the mind, once used to it, allows room to get round without conscious thought.

Dodgem car drivers are at an advantage in learning to steer. If you have never driven a dodgem, go to the nearest fairground and have some fun. Your car is not a dodgem but one can learn a lot from them.

Back in the car you can ask your teacher to keep a guiding hand on the wheel at first.

As you begin practising starts and stops also practise steering to the left and the right *while still in 1st gear*. Later, learn to steer with the right hand only – you will need to when changing gear and with the left hand only, so that it would be possible to make a hand signal.

Master one hand steering on an open space, not on the road, so that you will be accustomed to it. Apart from this practice and when you need one hand off for the above reasons, or working a switch, you *keep both hands on the wheel at all times*.

THE SMOOTH START FROM STANDING.

To move this stationary three quarters of a ton or so of metal may seem frightening but is not. The problem is to take all the steps correctly and at the right moment. I have, therefore, set them down in their correct order with drawings to help.

You are sitting correctly in the driver's seat, the mirrors adjusted for you (do them if you haven't already) and the handbrake holds the car. Your hands are correctly on the steering wheel (see page 27).

For the first time, you start to drive the car.

Key to Fig. 11.
1. Check that the gear lever is in neutral by moving it sideways about 2½″ along the neutral channel. *Proof* of being out of gear is that the lever moves *freely*. A way to be sure you are is to select two gears, say 1st and then 3rd, next checking

that you get back to neutral between them. Clutch down while doing this.

If you forget and start the engine in gear the car might jerk forward and hit somebody. *Whenever the engine is to be started, or re-started if it has stalled (stopped), this neutral check must be made.* On test the examiner will watch.

Key to Fig. 11.
2. Switch on the ignition, your teacher will show you how. Now start the engine. The switch may be incorporated in the ignition switch when a further turn of the key starts the engine, or it may be separate.

Immediately the engine runs release the switch. With practice your ear will tell you the instant the engine goes. At first your teacher can guide you. A wise novice will get his teacher to warm the engine for him first, so that when he comes to start it the engine will run sweetly and efficiently.

Never drive on a cold engine, it may stall at a "killer" moment. (See page 88).

USING THE CHOKE.
Starting a cold engine may require use of the choke control, sometimes automatic but usually a pull-knob on the dashboard, which can be kept out till the *earliest moment the engine runs normally,* when it is pushed home. Beware of leaving it out indefinitely. This could flood the engine with petrol and stall it – equally dangerous. If you keep your hand on it you won't forget. Your teacher can demonstrate the choke for you. If the engine won't start don't hold the starter switch on indefinitely. Rest a few seconds and try again with short bursts.

Key to Fig. 11.
3. Put the clutch pedal fully down (left foot) *and hold it.*

Key to Fig. 11.
4. Slip the gear lever to 1st (after your practice this will be easy) and *return your hand to the steering wheel.*

31

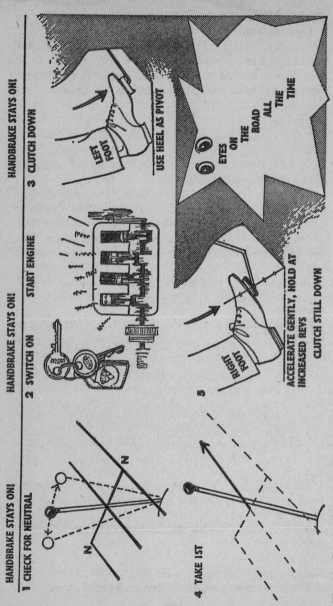

Fig. 11. Starting from standing, first five moves.

KEEP BOTH HANDS ON THE WHEEL.

Here, second only to the rule EYES ON THE ROAD, *is another* VITAL RULE. KEEP BOTH HANDS ON THE WHEEL WHENEVER POSSIBLE.

Later, on the road making a hand signal, usually with the right arm (to be discussed) you must not change gear at the same time because you would then have *no hands on the wheel*. This brings us to the second half of the rule: **WHEN BOTH HANDS CAN'T BE ON THE WHEEL AT LEAST ONE MUST BE.**

Hold the steering wheel as lightly as you would an egg but always ready to grip in emergency.

If you find difficulty in getting into 1st try: (a) Return to neutral and let the clutch up. Now press the pedal down and try again. (b) If this fails, press the clutch down and gently, without acceleration, try to get the lever in as you gradually allow the pedal partly up. At some point the lever should slip home. *Immediately, push the pedal down again (declutch)* to prevent the car moving. If you ever mistakenly select the wrong gear, especially reverse, this declutch procedure is the answer, quickly!

If these don't work, provided your space is flat, 2nd gear will do for starting. (When facing down-hill many good drivers use 2nd gear, as, helped by the decline, the engine will give sufficient power.)

Key to Fig. 11.

5. Now in gear with the clutch still down gently increase the revs. by accelerating. Press the accelerator (right foot) and about *a quarter* of its movement will be enough. You come to know by the engine's purr. (Starting up a hill requires more acceleration, and will be dealt with later).

The engine is now running at enough speed, *the clutch pedal is still down*, the gear in 1st. Your hands are on the wheel, in the correct position, holding it lightly. Your eyes are *in front*. The handbrake has been on, holding the car, all the time.

Key to Fig. 12.

1. The secret now is to allow the clutch pedal up only until

the biting point is reached and hold it there ready for 2 and 3.

The biting point is easily known if you listen to the purr of the engine. (Remember you are holding the accelerator at increased revs.)

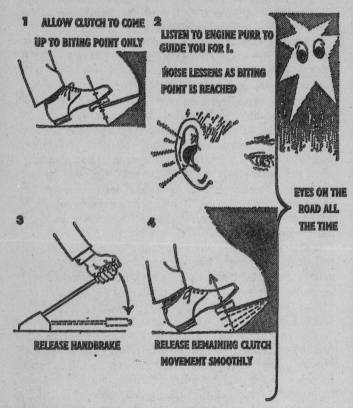

1   ALLOW CLUTCH TO COME UP TO BITING POINT ONLY

2   LISTEN TO ENGINE PURR TO GUIDE YOU FOR 1.

NOISE LESSENS AS BITING POINT IS REACHED

EYES ON THE ROAD ALL THE TIME

3   RELEASE HANDBRAKE

4   RELEASE REMAINING CLUTCH MOVEMENT SMOOTHLY

Fig. 12.   Starting from standing, next four moves.

Fig. 13 shows how your clutch pedal controls this operation. The clutch begins to "bite" between Fig. 13, C and E; the exact point depends on how the clutch plates are worn and varies from car to car.

The master key to holding the clutch where you want it is to keep your heel on the floor acting as a pivot.

34

Key to Fig. 12.
2. The engine's purring will die down when this point of clutch release is reached. Let the clutch up slowly so that you won't overshoot the biting point.

Think of this point as the moment of contact between neutral and the gears, between standing and moving. To be crude, between life and death, it's that important.

Learn well here. You will then have few worries in handling the car later, in parking, three-point turns etc. Your teacher can help you by placing his foot or hand over your foot on the clutch, until you have control.

The car is now straining to go but is held back by the hand brake.

Key to Fig. 12.
3. (a) You now let the handbrake off.

(b) **Maintain the clutch and accelerator positions as at 2.**

(c) Next fractionally let the clutch up, "slipping" it to allow only enough engine power for the road wheels to *begin* to move the car. The clutch plates, shown in fig. 3, page 20 are partially engaged.

Key to Fig. 12.
4. The more SMOOTHLY (not specially slowly) you now

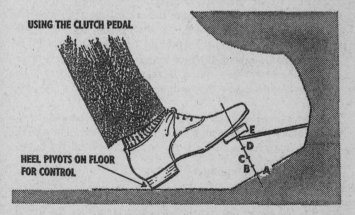

USING THE CLUTCH PEDAL

HEEL PIVOTS ON FLOOR FOR CONTROL

Fig. 13. The clutch begins to engage between C and E.

release the remaining movement in the clutch the better.

If you jerk your foot off or raise it too quickly the car will lurch forward and the engine may stall. Let it up steadily, in control, so that the car gains speed without jerks.

Further steady acceleration as the clutch passes D in fig. 13 (page 35) – clutch now fully engaged – increases speed as required till the maximum in 1st is reached.

LEARNING TO STOP.

1st gear is not normally used much beyond walking speed, when 2nd is engaged, but *before* you learn to change gear on the move or accelerate strongly *you must learn to stop*. Three-quarters of a ton of metal is lethal if you can't control it!

The exclamation mark is a serious one. *Until you can stop you must not go*.

After a few yards, *not miles*, learn to stop the car. Practise on your open space, starting, going a few yards and stopping, not once, but dozens of times until the "system" for stopping becomes instinctive. *It will be the life saver later*.

Here is the procedure.

BRAKING AT SLOW SPEEDS.

As you apply the footbrake the car will slow; just before stopping, the engine has to be disengaged from the road wheels, or it will stall. To prevent this the clutch pedal is depressed along with the foot brake and is *held* down. Once stopped, *before the clutch is released*, the handbrake is applied and the gear slipped into neutral, ready for the next start.

Don't forget – brake and clutch down to stop, once stopped, handbrake on, into neutral IN THAT ORDER. The clutch can then be released. Keep the footbrake on till the handbrake is applied.

THE FEET POSITIONS.

Fig. 14 shows the accepted feet positions after the initial start. The right foot is on the accelerator, the left lies beside the clutch ready for use at the next gear change or stop.

May I here spotlight the *danger* of driving in *heavy boots, gum boots or shoes that are muddy or greasy or have wet soles*? Tragedies happen so quickly that there *must never be any possibility of your feet getting "tied" up*, of one foot hitting two pedals, or of a shoe slipping from the brake, clutch (or accelerator) in emergency. Half seconds matter.

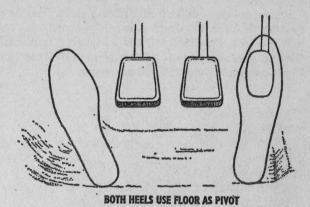

BOTH HEELS USE FLOOR AS PIVOT

Fig. 14. Feet positioned for normal driving.

Such dangers are part of the reasons for stressing the need to practise with the controls in a stationary car as your first essential task. Your feet need to be "tuned in" to their job.

The rule for stopping from any slow speed is BOTH FEET DOWN. Increasing the pressure on the footbrake progressively stops the car.

BRAKING AT FASTER SPEEDS.

Normally, from higher speeds, e.g. over 25 m.p.h., it is wrong to depress the clutch immediately; you wait till speed has dropped by braking, to about 10 m.p.h. before depressing it.

Now, more accustomed to the clutch and brake pedals, try an emergency stop on your teacher's unexpected snap command. This tunes up your reactions. Ask him to give you periodic snap commands.

Later, as you learn to use 2nd, 3rd and top gear, practise stops and emergency stops in each gear, before going on.

Ability to stop by instinct is essential. *No driver dare go onto a road with traffic until he has mastered stopping.* Get your emergency drill *sound* before attempting your first gear change.

EMERGENCY STOPS.

Emergency stops differ from ordinary stops. You forget the wait till 10 m.p.h. clutch down rule remembering only BOTH FEET FIRMLY DOWN as quickly as humanly possible. There is no time to think of when to press the clutch so you press both pedals. Fig. 15 shows you.

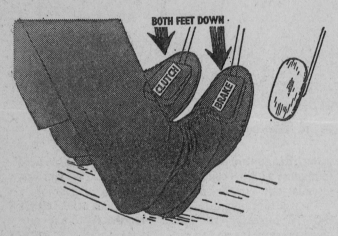

Fig. 15. Emergency stopping.

Even an emergency stop has to be controlled especially in any skiddy or dangerous conditions. It's useless "locking" the brakes and skidding. (Braking too hard causes "locking" and that means that the wheels stop turning and the car *slides*.) So avoid wet, skiddy weather or loose surfaces. Emergency stopping in skiddy conditions can be frightening. In skids *the car gets out of control* and even experienced drivers can be in trouble but this is dealt with later.

MILE-AN-HOUR DRIVING.

A superb exercise for your first live practice is to hold the clutch and accelerator pedals as at 1 – 2, fig. 12 page 34. Next let the handbrake off and drive ten or fifteen yards at a *mile-an-hour* or *barely moving*, controlling speed for this by fractional up or down movements of the clutch, but holding the accelerator steady. Practise till every inch you move takes a second and you will become master of the clutch. *This is the bread and butter of learning to drive well.*

These clutch exercises are vital but, due to friction, heat can wear the clutch. To avoid damage, never hold the clutch at the biting point longer than necessary and don't practise mile-an-hour driving for over 2 or 3 minutes at a time.

GEAR SPEEDS.

Now let's tackle gear changes still on the open space, though more room may be needed.

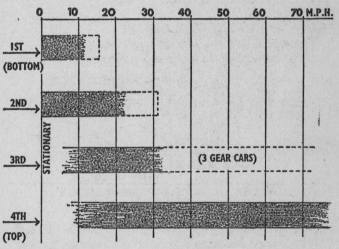

Fig. 16. Gear speeds.

Fig. 16 shows the speed ranges normally used in each gear; 1st gear for starting and up to 10 or 12 m.p.h.

If the car were facing downhill you could start in 2nd.

2nd takes the car up to about 20 m.p.h. 3rd accelerates

39

between 20 and 30 m.p.h. Top is taken for ordinary driving.

A learner need not race up to maximum speed in each gear, nor would that be expected. (In some cars 2nd is capable of up to 45 m.p.h. and 3rd to 70 m.p.h.) Fig. 16 is a guide for you.

Practise gear changes up and down on your open space. If you have a clear flat run of 250 yards you will find this ample to work your way through the gears to top and then stop. Travel short distances in each gear with just a little acceleration before changing up.

During these exercises you need not go above 20 m.p.h.

You will notice from fig. 16 that a car can pull away in 3rd (or top) from as low as 10 m.p.h. This is why there is no need for speed to do this exercise, and explains how it can be done in a short distance. If you have twice the space you will also be able to practise down gear changes.

On some cars a 5th gear to economise on petrol during higher speed cruising is fitted.

HOW TO CHANGE THE GEARS.

The gear is selected without hurry and once it is persuaded home the clutch is released in one *smooth* (not slow)

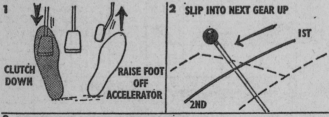

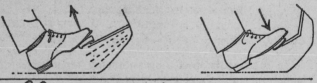

Fig. 17. Changing up the gears.

continuous movement. *Changing from gear to gear you do not pause while the clutch bites nor is the heel used as a pivot unless preferred.* Lift the foot entirely off the clutch pedal using your *thigh* muscles: the time it takes to say "zero" is enough. Re-accelerate promptly, don't dawdle or speed is lost.

Changing down is similar to changing up except that no acceleration follows the change if the lower gear is required to slow the car. This is referred to as "engine braking" and is used for slowing down or descending hills, to help hold the car back. Speed is controlled by the engine as well as the brakes. Fig. 18 shows changing down.

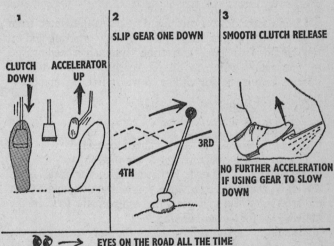

Fig. 18.   Changing down the gears.

When a change down is made to climb a hill or increase speed, re-accelerate as for changing up.

With experience you will find it unnecessary to press the clutch to the floor every time. If it goes well below the "biting point" that is enough.

EARLY OPEN SPACE TARGETS.

You now have an outline of early targets. Never keep at one exercise till tired; change to another. Most learners tire after an hour or two of tuition, so make that your daily limit.

The average reader should become confident to operate the controls after a few practice hours though the more technically minded may not need so long, but beware of over confidence. Drivers get used to one car so try and arrange to practise in the car you will use for the test.

MORE HELPFUL OPEN SPACE TRAINING EXERCISES.

Look at photographs 1 to 6 in the photograph section in the middle of the book. Here are the next few exercises to master; the captions explain them.

Obtain second hand cardboard boxes as illustrated from grocers etc. The lines can be made by tape or string laid on the ground. This "boxes and string" system has been proved of inestimable value to all the learners I have taught. Success here is the golden key to worry-free car manoeuvring.

REVERSING.

In these exercises you will soon need to reverse.

To pass the test good reversing is essential.

As walking backwards is harder than forwards, so is reversing. *But,* it is easier when you realise that, apart from the steering wheel and gear, the controls are used in the same way as for forward driving.

A smooth start in reverse needs the same care with the clutch and accelerator and you need the same ability to stop.

There is only one reverse gear in which you *never exceed walking pace*.

STOPPING IN REVERSE.

Remember the rule: BOTH FEET DOWN *for stopping when reversing*.

On some cars the brakes are less efficient in reverse so greater care is required and a longer distance needed to stop.

THE EYES WHEN REVERSING.

Fig. 19 shows the *vital* need for using the eyes. Develop fishy eyes for you must see all round. The shaded areas show where your eyes mainly have to watch. The heavier the shading the more care you need.

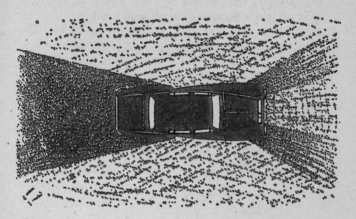

Fig. 19.   Where to look when reversing. Concentrate mainly where the shading is heaviest but do not ignore the lighter shaded areas.

In reversing straight back, the eyes must glance *rapidly* all over the place as well as behind. (Later, on the road or in confined places, your eyes will have to make frequent quick glances forward and to the sides as well as to the back to make sure you are not causing trouble to other road users or hitting anything. This explains the lighter shading to the front and sides of the car.)

On the road as opposed to your open space, children or low objects such as mini-bikes are a common danger. Accidents in reverse are often minor (hitting a pillar, kerb etc.) but can be serious. A van driver I knew killed his child accidentally, by reversing "blind". *So take care.*

Don't put your head out of the window but turn it well round and look out of the back window over your inside (left) shoulder. In this position you can see a little out of the side window as well. Get your shoulders right round, as far as you can but retaining control of the foot pedals.

It makes things easier and safer to twist round and get your eyes on the main target. *Keep both hands on the wheel.* You may see drivers who put their left arm along the top of the seat. Don't.

STEERING IN REVERSE.

Many learners become flustered wondering how to turn the steering to reverse in the direction they want. The task will be easy if you keep fig. 20 pictured in your mind.

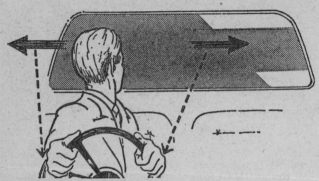

PULL DOWN LEFT TO GO LEFT, RIGHT TO GO RIGHT

Fig. 20. Picture this figure in your memory to remind you which hand to pull on when steering in reverse.

The eyes are trained behind for reversing but quick frequent glances to the front and sides, including over your right shoulder, have to be made for safety. Fig. 19 shows the areas to concentrate on and fig. 21 gives an example of why. Greater car control is needed in reversing.

The reason is the danger of "swinging wide" explained· below which is also one reason for the forward and sideways glances.

Re-study fig. 10 on page 29. If you reverse from 1 to 2 the rear of the car, now leading, "cuts" the corner as before, while the steering (front) wheels now at the "back" of the car, swing round the wider arc again. That is, the path of the wheels is identical, but reversed.

You have to watch that the front of the car, *swinging*

wider as it does, won't hit something (just as you have to watch that the back doesn't "cut" a corner – mounting the kerb when going forwards).

Fig. 21 shows a driver taking his position in a car park. A, B and C are typical danger points.

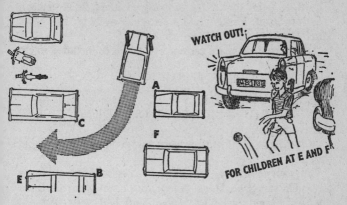

Fig. 21. Danger in a car park.

You've got the theory – now train with the exercises. See photographs 1 to 6.

Be unafraid (at slow speed, of course) to spin the steering During these tight manoeuvres. A lock to lock turn should be possible at a mile-an-hour speed while the car moves only a few feet.

Practise at low speed. Use superb clutch control by "slipping" the clutch where necessary.

While you must not turn the wheel of a stationary car you can start the "spinning" movement – *which gets the results* – from the instant movement begins.

For reversing in a straight line between the two strings, you won't need to slip the clutch much. Slipping would be required if you had to slow and start again e.g. to rectify bad steering.

On test you will probably be asked to reverse into a side-road opening from one side or, perhaps both. The three point turn, another test requirement also needs good reversing.

45

In your initial training stop the car and get out to have a look. You may be surprised to see that things are not as you thought.

CAR CONTROL TESTS ON "TEST".

The three point turn. Stop properly at kerb. Road camber. The turn itself. Reverse into a side-road opening. The uphill start. Downhill starts. Hill parking.

These are three main car control exercises included in the test:

THREE POINT TURN
REVERSE INTO A SIDE-ROAD OPENING
HILL START

Make the mastery of these your first goal, towards passing the test.

Get your teacher to take the car to suitable quiet places for each exercise. Then, when you have won all three "battles", conquered car control and had your first experience on a road with traffic – you should be ready for general driving, dealt with later.

I STRESS THAT YOU LEARN THE THREE POINT TURN, REVERSE INTO A SIDE-ROAD AND THE HILL START FIRST. SOME TEACHERS AND PUPILS ARE TEMPTED TO DO ORDINARY TRAFFIC DRIVING FIRST. VERY SILLY. AT THIS STAGE YOU ARE A MENACE ON BUSY ROADS BUT AFTER SOME HOURS OF LEARNING THESE DIFFICULT MANOEUVRES YOU WILL HAVE GAINED IMMENSELY IN KNOWLEDGE AND CONFIDENCE.

THE THREE POINT TURN.

(Making the car face the opposite way in a quiet road without using a side-road.)

Get your teacher to drive you to a safe road e.g. a cul-de-sac about 25 feet wide with pavements on both sides.

You need to be specially aware of other traffic.

Don't start a three point turn if another car is approaching but let it pass. If you are in the middle of the turn and can wait at the point you have reached, to let any approaching vehicle go by, do so.

You only attempt a three point turn if the road is clear both ways and never near a corner or where cars are liable to come fast. Commonsense!

The three point or three move turn is only possible if the road is wide enough; if, on test, the examiner picks too narrow a road and you need five moves don't worry. It won't be held against you. All you are expected to do is to turn the car in the least possible number of forward and backward moves, without hitting the kerb either side and without, as far as possible, inconveniencing others.

At the start, the car should be next to the kerb on your side of the road; at the finish it should be facing the other way, parked next to the kerb on the other side.

Eight of the photographs (5 to 12) in the middle of the book, reveal most of the secrets of a masterly three point turn.

STOP PROPERLY AT THE KERB.

On test and normally when you pull in, do so correctly. finishing only a few inches (not over 12 inches) from, and parallel to, the kerb. The examiner will be impressed if you do this and when you come to the three point turn you will be ready to begin.

Remember to pull on the handbrake and be in neutral before releasing the clutch. Keep the engine running, when on test, unless asked to switch off.

Form the habit of good parking for these reasons and so that your car will not inconvenience traffic and is less likely to be damaged.

ROAD CAMBER.

Fig. 22 is a worm's eye view of a "cambered" road – higher in the middle than the edges, to allow rainwater to drain.

If there is any camber, in the three point turn, you need superb clutch control, already learnt if you have done your homework! You must release the handbrake at each "standing start", just at the vital moment the clutch begins to

47

bite, otherwise the car may run into the gutter and the wheels hit the kerb. The penalties could be *test failure* and *damage to the tyre which could cause* a fatal accident. If you hit a kerb get your tyres checked by an expert at once. It can also damage steering. Have steering checked after any severe blow.

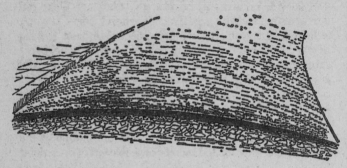

Fig. 22.   Worms's eye view of a road showing the camber.

The damage can be – although it is not usually – extensive and may not be visible on the outside of the tyre. It depends on the impact and the state of the tyre. It may result in an unexpected burst tyre thousands of miles later. You can't practise tyre bursts but be prepared by reading part three for life saving tips.

THE TURN ITSELF.

(Our step by step instructions assume that you are correctly positioned by the kerb.) Look again at photographs 5 to 12.

Check both ways that all is clear. *Turn round and look behind* as well as in the mirrors.

If all clear take first gear and start forward at a mile-an-hour or less.

Immediately the car is in motion again check for traffic and if safe, *swing the steering into full lock* to take you towards the other side.

You must be in full lock within the first three or four feet of movement. Then you go a little quicker but still *slowly* towards the other side, checking for safety all the time.

After your open space practice stopping with the wheels near the string (see photographs 5 and 6), you should know how near you can go to the other side without hitting the kerb.

During the last *three* to *four* feet to this point, you slow down to barely moving, and then, *but not before*, you swing the steering back to the other lock. Stop with the nose (bumpers) about a foot from the kerb. You stop with the steering already in the opposite lock (you have just put it there) ready for the reverse to the side you came from. Much practice needed.

Next, handbrake on, gear into neutral, and look both ways to be sure all is clear.

You now do a smooth reverse backwards, remembering to get the whole upper part of your body, head and neck round, so that you can see where you are aiming. All the time be alert for approaching traffic; with skill you will be able to manage quick glances up and down the road during the period between leaving one kerb and approaching the other.

Keep *fully* in this second lock till the back bumpers are 3 to 4 feet off the kerb.

Once again it is *only in these last three or four feet, not before* that you swing back to the original steering lock, *ready to go forward*. Stop with the rear bumpers about a foot from the kerb. The examiner will not want you to allow the bumpers over the pavement.

Don't be afraid to spin the steering wheel to get these lock changes. The car, as it nears the kerb must be only just moving while you change lock. The *slower* the *easier* and watch you don't cross the hands on the wheel.

At this point handbrake on and into neutral, with continual checks both ways for danger.

If safe, you drive forward pulling up on the other side, correctly as you did before the turn was started.

Sometimes, with experience, on a fairly wide road, you will realise that about *half way* across during the backwards move, you *could* go forward and round from there. If so, do. On test, you will probably find you need all the road available to make the turn in three. So, with your teacher, practise in a "difficult" road.

The three point turn needs skill, repeated practice and above all fishy eyes, all the time, for safety. Study the relevant photographs 5 to 12 and practise often. It is useless going for the test till you master this.

REVERSE INTO A SIDE-ROAD OPENING.

The examiner will ask you to reverse into a limited opening. He normally stops you well before the side-road and explains what he wants you to do. You should reverse down the middle of the opening if it is too narrow to merit keeping to one side. If it is wider you would keep about 2–3 feet from your side,

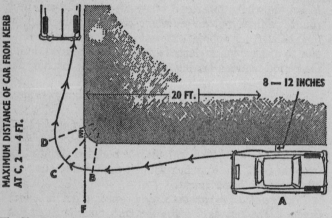

Fig. 23. Reversing into a limited opening on the nearside (passenger's side).

You are expected to reverse round the pavement or edge keeping within 2 or 3 feet of your own side. (Note: Learners taking the test in small vans are usually asked to reverse from the offside (see fig. 24), and having pulled in at Z are asked to move to A before beginning.)

Find suitable quiet places with your teacher taking the car there and *practise and practise until you are proficient*.

The snag is to keep clear of and not hit the edge. (Rasping

the tyre along a pavement edge is one of the worst treatments you can give it.)

Your homework with the cartons should have helped. If you reversed through the boxes efficiently, and know how far from the pavement the inside wheels are, this will be almost child's play.

The worry is about other traffic and you must flash your eyes all the time in every direction from which danger *could* come. Get lots of road condition practice in quiet streets.

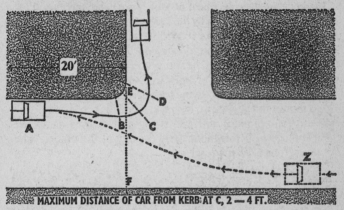

MAXIMUM DISTANCE OF CAR FROM KERB AT C, 2 — 4 FT.

Fig. 24. Reversing into a limited opening on the offside (driver's side).

Assume you have pulled up correctly by the kerb at A – say 20 feet from the opening (figs. 23 and 24). Under superb clutch and accelerator control, reverse towards B, having checked all round, especially behind, for traffic. As you approach B ease the car from the kerb but not so suddenly or acutely that one of the *front (steering) wheels*, swinging wide mounts it (see page 44). Between B and D the whole car is only 2 or at the most 4 feet from the kerb.

Go dead slowly at B. You will soon see down the road you are to enter. You may need temporarily to move forward to allow someone out of the opening.

The line of the opening's pavement – if extended imaginarily into the road you are leaving, would pass through both of your rear wheels (illustrated by a dotted line EF in figs. 23 and 24).

Check for traffic, glance all ways; especially watch the road you are leaving and if forced to stop, *no harm done*.

From position B, when that imaginary line would pass through the rear wheels, *barely moving*, you keep the car parallel to the kerb as it rounds away from you.

Swing the wheel into lock (as much as required – probably immediate full lock) as you move slowly between B and C. Towards D you straighten again (don't be afraid to really swing that steering wheel *at slow speed*) and carry on till the car is running parallel to the kerb. You aim to stop after 20 – 40 ft. having steered in to within a foot of the kerb, unless the examiner asks you to carry on; or, you could ask first, how far down the road he wants you to go.

If your judgement of *when* to swing into lock is poor the answer is practise. To swing too early causing the back wheel to mount the pavement, is as bad a fault as too late.

If your practice with the string and cartons has proved insufficient for this manoeuvre (or any of the others) *return to it. Homework matters!*

THE UPHILL START.

Before you can uphill-start, understand this:

Provided acceleration is enough to move the car forward with the brakes off, there is one point of contact, at which the clutch pedal can be held, which stops the car rolling back downhill (handbrake off), but at which the gear is insufficiently engaged (because the clutch is not fully released) to move the car uphill. You are, as it were, suspended between going and rolling back.

You learned to use this point of contact in the smooth start. You already know about waiting till this point is reached before releasing the handbrake.

The difference in the hill-start is in the *amount* of acceleration.

More petrol is needed to make the car climb. You press the accelerator perhaps half as much again as normal. If you overdo it the engine will roar which is wrong. You would rarely press it more than three-quarters down.

Find a quiet hill and experiment till you can hold the car *still* – neither going forward nor rolling back – in 1st gear with the handbrake *off*. This proves that you can do it.

Once you achieve this correct "balance" between accelerator and clutch *every time*, your task is done. You should be able to start and accelerate off as if there was no hill and without fuss.

The first time you practise uphill starts, the car will probably run back. *Stop it with the footbrake* (and clutch down); *pull on the handbrake* and *begin again*.

Fig. 25. Hill starts. Practise first on slight inclines, then progress to steeper hills.

Don't try wild acceleration or jumping off the clutch which result in a muddle. *Stop and re-start.* It is essential that you don't practise with anyone behind you, you could easily run back. It's the old faithful, commonsense. *If she runs back, stop dead.* Don't be sad if you fail, just keep on till you succeed. Once mastered (and master it you must for the test) no hill should worry you.

Note: For the special "Hill Start" on test; moving off procedure, shown by fig. 29 and described by text in part II, must also be followed. A signal, for example, is required and to be able to give it by hand, if asked, needs practice.

On a hill you may find the gear won't go in; when you have tried the tips on page 33, try this: Only if safe behind,

53

release the handbrake a little but be ready to stop with the footbrake and allow the car to slip back about ½". This usually works.

DOWNHILL STARTS.

The downhill start is as easy as the uphill is tricky but there are pitfalls. Commonsense again; sorry to stress it, but if you keep it in mind that that is all there is in driving, it helps reduce arch-enemy fear. You begin on slight declines as with the uphill start and progress to steeper ones.

The car moves itself if the brake is released but it is less simple than that. Freewheeling downhill is unsafe as control would rest only with the brake. Brakes can fail, but more of such situations in part four, for the moment remember you *must never freewheel but keep the car in control with a gear engaged when moving*.

You therefore take a gear and as usual let the clutch up smoothly but with little or no acceleration. Let the handbrake off as the biting point is reached. Thus, you increase your control over the car. It is normal to use 2nd gear for a downhill start.

Once going you may find you need to accelerate more or not, depending on the steepness of the slope. Being in gear provides "engine braking" and prevents the car freewheeling away. In a low gear you may not require the footbrake and as the decline lessens you take 3rd gear and so on.

Similarly, in general driving, on *approaching* a steep hill

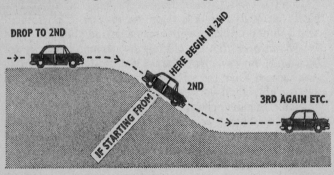

Fig. 26. Using the gears going down hills.

down you take a lower gear to increase control and a lower gear still if the hill is steep. It is best to take the lowest gear you think you need beforehand at the top of the hill. You may also need to brake. 2nd would be the lowest gear normally required.

Fig. 26 shows the use of the gears going downhill.

The use of gears to tackle the problem of losing speed going up hills will be dealt with later in part two. See page 69.

HILL PARKING.

To park on a hill the car should be parallel to the kerb and not more than 6″ from it. The handbrake should be securely on.

Fig. 27.   Parking on a hill.

Facing downhill.

It is vital that the front wheels should be turned in (but not touching) so that if the handbrake failed the car would be quickly stopped by the kerb. For extra safety put the gear in reverse.

Facing uphill.

The front wheels are turned outwards so that, rolling back, they would "swing wide" and be stopped by the kerb; leave the gear in 1st for uphill safety. Fig. 27 illustrates.

YOU can prevent the runaway cars one hears about.

Part Two

General Road And Traffic Driving

BEGINNING ON THE ROAD

Get experience. Study all of the book before driving. Checking the doors. A running commentary. Concentration. Notes for teachers. Mirrors. More about stopping in emergency. Emergency stop "on test".

GET EXPERIENCE.

By now you should be competent to start on the road.

To pass the test there is no substitute for miles of experience. Seize every opportunity of gaining it but don't overdo it; an hour at a time is enough as beginners tire easily – *without realising it.*

STUDY ALL OF THIS BOOK BEFORE DRIVING ON THE ROAD.

There is an obvious danger when you start general road driving – you might meet a tricky situation you don't understand. This, alas, could happen in the first few miles. You need to know the written, and the unwritten, rules. That is one reason for studying the rest of the book now. So carry on with your "homework" *and conquer the theory of driving. Win this battle and the road will be easier.* Your teacher will be there to guide you but with fore-knowledge, you will understand his "language" better.

CHECKING THE DOORS.

The driver must *always* check *all* the doors are shut. He alone is responsible. The surest way is to walk round the car and look. Examiners like to see care taken.

A RUNNING COMMENTARY.

You can learn a lot from an expert's running commentary.

Get your teacher or friends to explain why they do things as they drive and try to learn from the commentary what you would be worrying about if driving. What are the dangerous situations? Why are they dangerous? Where your eyes should concentrate in picking out dangers; how you can anticipate them; what speeds are safe in which conditions; how early does one begin positioning for turns; when and why do you need to change gear or start braking; all about signals; how far ahead should your eyes range; how to tackle traffic lights, one ways, roundabouts, etc?

From this I hope you will realise how you need to think ahead – all the time – on what you should direct the bulk of your concentration.

Ask Questions! You may spot a fault in the teacher's driving of which he was unaware! If he has not done this before he may be surprised how much it *helps him realize which things he now does instinctively that you will need to be taught.*

CONCENTRATION.

Your concentration on the road must always be spot on. In concentrating try to avoid becoming tense. Don't keep at it for too long for tenseness increases; your aim is to achieve relaxed concentration. Beware of over-concentrating so that your teacher's comments, or *commands*, pass unheard.

NOTES FOR TEACHERS.

A teacher *must never lose his temper*. If a teacher can't get on with his pupil let him find a new instructor.

When a difficulty needs explanation draw in to the side, traffic permitting, and discuss it without being worried by traffic.

Many teachers fit an *extra* mirror so they can instruct the learner taking account of traffic behind without having to look round.

The teacher must be ready in an emergency to grasp control. He must anticipate where his pupils reactions may be slow or his judgement *wrong*.

Explain to the pupil that you may at times have to step on the clutch or knock the gear out and seize the handbrake;

that if you have to control the steering you will do so with your right hand and *must be allowed free charge*, but he should keep his hands at the wheel ready to have it back. If the open space work has been done none of these measures may be needed.

For difficult pupils, a dual control unit, covering brake or clutch, or both, should be fitted. They cost a few pounds depending on the car and can be fitted by a garage. Automobile and Industrial Developments Ltd. of Sydenham, London, S.E.26 make such units.

MIRRORS.

You saw how to adjust these in part one. Get used to flashing your eyes to the mirror(s) frequently. See in an instant what is behind, then *eyes back to the road*. Does someone want to pass or slip through on your inside? Is there a fast sports model a few places behind which may soon flash by you? Mirror watching is an art to be developed. If, however, you dwell too long on the mirror you will be in an accident in front.

The majority of the time your eyes must be on the road. That is the vital message.

Your teacher must be watchful while you learn your mirror-to-road eye switching. Learn to move the eyes fast as indicated in fig. 28. Up to the centre mirror and back to the road, then having re-assessed the road ahead, you may need to check the side mirror(s) and *back to the road*.

Never "fix" the eyes on the mirror. No need to know what shape of girl driver is behind, only if a car is there and how close.

Aim to know at all times what is behind. Form a running picture, as it were, in your mind. Do this in town and country. It needs regular glances but if you value your life I repeat, *the majority of the time concentrate in front*.

There are reasons for this *continuous* knowledge.

(a) To be able to judge how early or if safe, to ease out to pass a stationary car, or turn right without being hemmed in or hit by an overtaking vehicle. If someone is pressing on your tail you can give an early right signal to forewarn him not to pass or move in and slow to let him go on.

CORRECT USE OF THE MIRROR, IS THE SECRET,
WHICH ENABLES YOU TO POSITION YOURSELF
CORRECTLY SO THAT TRAFFIC BEHIND KNOWS
YOUR INTENTION.

(b) You will know of cars, or motor bikes which can be
hidden in the blind spots, as they are unlikely to have been
hidden all the time over several miles. Fig. 2 shows the blind
areas.

(c) You will know when you are being passed. Don't swing
out or accelerate, and slow down if necessary.

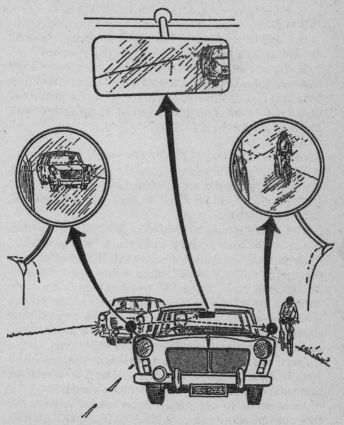

Fig. 28.   Split second mirror glances behind.

Get your teacher to ask you from time to time, what is behind. If on the ball you will be able to reply before having another check.

MORE ABOUT STOPPING IN EMERGENCY.

In part one you were practising emergency stops almost from the beginning. *On the road remember these extra points:*

In a desperate emergency there is no time for a mirror check and stopping may be everything; you should have done your mirror work, not needing to check behind.

If you stop suddenly and are hit by a following vehicle, you should be clear in law, but what if the jerk of the crash has broken your neck – whiplash action, as it is termed?

So know what is behind; in a real emergency one might have to risk being hit; but it should never happen if the driver following is good. You may have an option, for instance of going onto a grass verge, instead of stopping suddenly, knowing you may be hit.

EMERGENCY STOP "ON TEST".

The examiner will arrange a signal with you for when he wants you to demonstrate an emergency stop. He may slap the dashboard or other signal. Practise with your teacher, using a similar signal.

The instant he signals *both feet firmly down and stop.* No delay; it's your reaction speed that's being tested, *but,* commonsense again, keep it controlled. If it's wet and you feel the car slide, the wheels will have locked, so release the brake a little for a split second and then reapply firm pressure but not so hard as to lock the wheels again. Practice with your teacher is the only way to learn to do a properly controlled emergency stop every time. Once stopped, handbrake on, gear out. On test the examiner will tell you what to do next. My advice is don't just sit there or you may be hit from behind! You could ask the examiner if he wishes you to draw in or continue. Remember to stop completely.

Knowing how to stop without losing control may one day save your life. Look at part 4, SKIDS WHEN BRAKING HARD.

Moving off. Ordinary two way roads. How fast should I go? Road narrows. A golden rule. Country lanes. Hooting. Hairpin bends. Turning into a steep opening. Dual carriageways.

MOVING OFF.

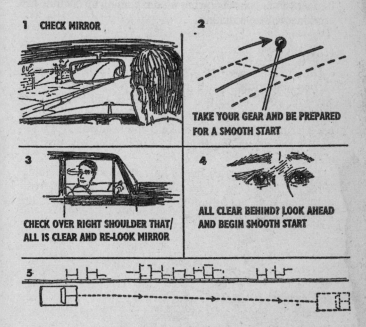

1 CHECK MIRROR

2 TAKE YOUR GEAR AND BE PREPARED FOR A SMOOTH START

3 CHECK OVER RIGHT SHOULDER THAT/ ALL IS CLEAR AND RE-LOOK MIRROR

4 ALL CLEAR BEHIND? LOOK AHEAD AND BEGIN SMOOTH START

5 TAKE ABOUT 40 YARDS TO REACH NORMAL DISTANCE FROM KERB

Fig. 29. Moving off from the kerbside. Use signal if traffic about and remember to cancel it.

Key to Fig. 29.

A right signal during (1), (2) and (3) is required to warn following traffic. Cancel it as soon as you are off. If the examiner asks for a hand signal you would give it during (3) but withdraw it and return hand to the wheel before (4).

61

At (5) pick up speed smartly, not ferociously. While picking up speed watch mirror for cars appearing behind and be guided by it.

When parked behind another parked car you must pull out more sharply than in (5) and may also need to wait because of *oncoming* traffic. You are likely to be asked to do this by the examiner so practise well before the test. Don't forget your mirror work and hand signal or flasher. The frequent error is not knowing what is coming up behind. The examiner will be watching.

ORDINARY TWO-WAY ROADS.

On ordinary two-way roads keep to your own side, driving about four or five feet out but not so close that the the tyres could pick up stones etc. Once embedded in the tyre, flints can cause punctures later. There is also danger to pedestrians and of hitting the kerb and losing control (even at slow speeds) and bursting a tyre or damaging your steering.

Road widths vary so this is only an approximate guide. Your normally keep in the middle of *your half* of the road but where your half has room for two lanes keep well to the left to allow for overtakers.

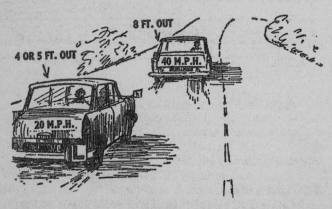

Fig. 30. Distance from kerb in relation to speed.

HOW FAST SHOULD I GO?

On test, where safe, you should pick up to reasonable speed. Exceeding 50 m.p.h. would, however, be unwise, as would dawdling at 20 m.p.h. for no reason.

You will learn to keep up with the traffic stream (unless it is too fast) BUT *never* exceed a speed limit, or, failure!

After passing the test you may want to go faster. You then keep further from the kerb. If width permits say 7 feet at 40 m.p.h. and 10 feet at 65 m.p.h., giving extra safety in case of need. A car is far more difficult to control, *especially to stop*, at high speeds so room is essential. If the road is not wide enough for speed you can bet that to drive fast is dangerous. Until you have done 100,000 miles *remember you are still inexperienced*, so avoid speed.

To illustrate, fig. 30 shows a learner doing 20 m.p.h. and an experienced driver, who has just overtaken, 40 m.p.h. Don't be so far out that you endanger oncoming traffic. The narrower the road the lower the speed.

Keep a steady path, avoid wandering and don't court death by looking at scenery, a frequent fault!

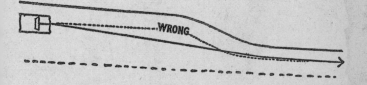

Fig. 31. Road narrows. Ease out early.

ROAD NARROWS.

Many roads narrow without warning. On such it's a dangerous habit to come out suddenly as indicated by the dotted line, fig. 31. The solid arrow shows how you ease out smoothly well in advance.

A GOLDEN RULE.

DO NOT DRIVE AT A SPEED FROM WHICH YOU CAN'T STOP, IN THE PREVAILING ROAD CON-

DITIONS, WITHIN THE DISTANCE YOU CAN SEE IS CLEAR. (OR IS GOING TO BE CLEAR.)

Never forget this golden rule and continually *remind yourself to abide by it*. Check yourself if you find speed becoming your master. Accidents happen quickly and unexpectedly. A split second is too long to describe accident "duration".

COUNTRY LANES.

Fig. 32 shows a driver U, on a country lane. Often these are so narrow that passing places are provided but even on wider lanes be extra alert. On lanes you keep closer in than normal, maybe only a foot from the edge. Go slowly and remember the golden rule, for there is little accident evasion margin!

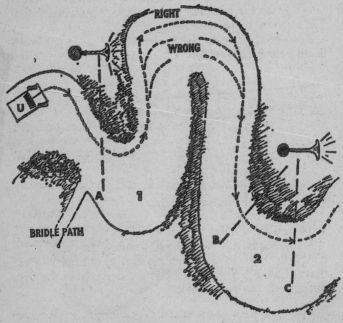

Fig. 32. A narrow country lane.

But! The "other chap" may not be following the rule. He may be a countryman who uses the lane a lot and rarely finds anyone on it. Carelessness has crept in and he may "cut" over to your side at corners, 1 and 2, driving fast.

HOOTING.

Providing you keep in and *hoot* at the danger points A, B and C you should have alerted him. Your hoot must not be just a touch but long enough and *correctly timed*, to be heard. A hoot does *not* mean you take less care (some people are deaf). Avoid cutting corners yourself; the dotted lines marked WRONG show this common pitfall.

Accident insurance claim forms usually have a question "Did you sound your horn?" which shows the importance experts attach to this safety measure. Don't listen to those who say in some countries or in some towns abroad, horns are prohibited. Such places do not have our weight of traffic or our lanes and conditions.

Another typical question is "Were you on the correct side of the road?" Experienced drivers may cut corners they can see round but you should not. Examiners would frown on such techniques being used by beginners.

Note the bridle path shown in fig. 32, a frequent danger spot on lanes, as are gateways, driveways etc. from any of which kids may shoot out on bicycles, "soapbox" carts etc. If you killed a child, by speeding along a narrow road, as quickly as you might swat a fly, WOULDN'T YOUR CONSCIENCE BLEED?

Anything can happen, *including the incredible*. Give a hoot at danger points and control your speed mania.

I stress do not rely on the horn. It won't clear the road. Imagine a herd of cows at a blind bend. They keep coming regardless! One usually has to stop to let them walk round. Give animals ample room and be prepared, by taking blind bends slowly under 100% control.

HAIRPIN BENDS.

You may meet roads which have hairpin bends where the corner angle is under 90°. They are often on hills – the devil making things difficult! The secret is to change down, whether on hills or flat, probably to 2nd gear, reaching the corner at walking speed.

Should speed drop on an uphill so that you need 1st gear the change from 2nd can usually be made smartly once below walking pace. If it won't go in you have to stop, pull on the handbrake *firmly* and do a hill start.

Keep well in to your own side, whether a left or right bend. Cutting a corner on a right bend could fail you.

Remember to hoot on blind bends.

"I can't get round in one go! What can I do?" Answer: stop, *before* reaching the wrong side of the road, reverse a little (check behind) to straighten and forward again. You may require several manoeuvres, unless there is no traffic for miles when you can go over a bit onto the "wrong" side.

TURNING INTO A STEEP OPENING.

On test, you may have to make a right or left turn into a steep uphill. As you will be almost stationary on entering, you need considerable acceleration to get you up. If you can find a place like this, practise with your teacher. It's difficult.

For a steep downhill opening, control with the brake and gear (usually 2nd), changing up when the hill levels.

DUAL CARRIAGEWAYS.

On dual (one way traffic) carriageways keep to the left lane to let faster drivers overtake. If you need to pass a vehicle move to the outer lane (or the middle lane if three) I deal more fully with overtaking later. Lanes are often marked but if not you assume them. *Others expect you to.* Where "cats' eyes" exist there is no danger in driving on them if need arises.

FOLLOWING OTHERS

Thinking time. The gap to leave. Leaving room for others to overtake. Braking from speed. Seeing beyond the car in front. Warning people behind. The gears in traffic. The gears for going uphill. Rain and wet.

THINKING TIME.

If the car in front stops suddenly, can you?

There is a time lag between the moment the chap in front brakes (or hits something) and your reaction – the thinking time gap. His brakes may also be better than yours. *You must leave ample space between you and the vehicle in front to allow thinking and braking time.*

In traffic hold ups if the queue moves only a little at a time the gap need be as little as 15 feet between pull-ups, closing to 5 feet when stopped. Leave extra space at uphill stops lest the car in front slips back.

At each stop of more than seconds use your handbrake and go out of gear. Take 1st again immediately before moving.

As traffic speeds up, increase the gap, especially if the long view ahead is hidden, for example, if you have a van in front. If you can see ahead it is safer because you can usually anticipate when the man in front is likely to stop.

Adjust the gap as conditions dictate – the life blood message; longer for narrow or busy places, blind bends, obstructions, if near walkers etc. – safer a little closer on open roads.

THE GAP TO LEAVE.

At 20 m.p.h. leave 4 or 5 car lengths, at 40 m.p.h. 9 to 11. At 50 m.p.h. or over you must leave far, far more. The term car lengths is approximate, leave lots of room. As a learner your reactions will be slow and the experienced can often take avoiding action which you can't. Show-off (or ignorant) nose-to-tail driving is the cause of many disgraceful pile-ups.

LEAVING ROOM FOR OTHERS TO OVERTAKE.

As stream speed increases allow those in front away unless your wish is to overtake. A long gap is needed for thinking and braking time but you must also leave space for faster traffic to pass.

If a bunch of selfish drivers, who don't follow this rule, forms, faster cars can only pass at risk to themselves and you.

If a line of cars is caught behind a lorry, on a too narrow road, they may have to plod along for miles. All must be patient and wait for a safe time to pass. If the driver immediately behind the lorry has a slow car he should drop back allowing faster cars to "leap-frog" him one by one as they pass the lorry. Consideration for others is the essence of good driving.

BRAKING FROM SPEED.

Braking at speed is hazardous even with perfect brakes because the car's momentum (weight multiplied by speed) acts increasingly against you. If the brakes are poor or badly adjusted (rarely evident at lower speeds) the danger is magnified and deadly. Bad brakes can unbalance a car "throwing" it to one side. *Any maladjustment must be put right.*

Get your teacher to demonstrate, on a dry day at a safe place, the long distance needed to stop from high speed. *Especially long distances are required downhill.*

SEEING BEYOND THE CAR IN FRONT.

Try not to follow directly in line but drive, if possible, slightly to one side, to enable you to see round and ahead for danger. The greater your "following" gap the better the visibility and the *less hidden you are from oncomers.* Particularly, it helps you to see cyclists that the man in front, and you, will have to move out to pass.

WARNING PEOPLE BEHIND.

As the brake lights of a vehicle in front go on, you press your brake pedal lightly or as required. This puts on your brake-lights warning anyone behind. If the slowing up is slight, you have lost nothing but in an emergency:

(a) you are ready "covering" the brake pedal and

(b) the driver behind has been warned.

Sometimes you will see the brake lights of a car several places ahead come on and be able to warn those behind you, even before a less alert driver immediately ahead of you has acted!

If a stream is stopping, say, at a zebra crossing, also give a hand slowing down signal. If you feel the zebra will be empty before you reach it and you may not need to stop, change down, withdrawing the hand signal while you do so, thus being geared to go ahead from a slow speed.

Your hand *signal alerts both following and oncoming traffic*, who may not know your intentions. It is especially good if you are heading a stream but less vital at lights, where the change to red is obvious. It will please the examiner but only do it when you have time to do so comfortably.

To avoid accidents at hazards it is your *priority duty* to keep *both hands on the wheel* (you might have to swerve). This applies on test as in everyday driving and no examiner would expect otherwise. That is why you only hand signal if there is time. For hand signals and their timing see page 102.

THE GEARS IN TRAFFIC.

Study fig. 16. A car can pull away in top from as low as 20 m.p.h. or in 3rd from 10 m.p.h. If in a stream in top when everyone has to slow to 25 m.p.h. probably no-one will drop a gear for quick acceleration so as you cannot accelerate rapidly, it is correct to pick up speed gradually without changing. 3rd gear can be used from low speeds where it is unnecessary to drop to 2nd and 2nd can be used from a crawl. *For quicker acceleration do change down.* Should traffic drop to a snail's pace *without stopping*, depress the clutch and immediately raise it to the "slipping" point (see page 35). The car is moving in 2nd gear and thus you can keep crawling but ready to speed up. *Practise the technique.*

THE GEARS FOR GOING UPHILL.

When losing speed uphill take a lower gear early and increase acceleration rapidly to keep going. If the engine "labours" change down at once. Labouring produces a metalic tinkling noise called "pinking". Your teacher should demonstrate.

RAIN AND WET.

IN WET WEATHER LEAVE TWO OR THREE TIMES THE STOPPING SPACE REQUIRED FOR DRY CONDITIONS AND REDUCE SPEEDS IN GENERAL BY ONE THIRD OR MORE.

Ice and snow are dealt with in part four.

Training your eyes. Two "experts" tips. More refined road reading.

TRAINING YOUR EYES.

In fig. 33, A represents your eyes. K is where most learners wrongly concentrate. Some allow their eyes to wander to the scenery L. Such people will not live long.

To keep your eyes on the road is not enough; the beginner has to learn to flash or switch his eyes at speed. This switching, ranging over a wide area, becomes possible with practice and is a tonic for the eyes. At slow speeds, the view should range a quarter of a mile ahead. Above 40 m.p.h. vision should cover up to three quarters of a mile or more where possible.

If there are no pedestrians probably Fig. 33 K, where the beginner centres his gaze, is the safest area. He should cover this part instinctively while his eyes switch far and wide, rapidly, so that no changing traffic situation is missed.

The avoidance of danger is the heart of safety.

The eyes should anticipate a door opening at B and someone jumping onto the road (the car should be steered a door's width clear of parked cars to allow for this); they ought to have seen path J and been sure no runaway horse or child cyclist was emerging, as has happened to me.

The driver ought to know a wagon is at D ready to turn left and be sure it has managed to stop. E is a wet patch he might not be able to pick out till later.

At C the motor cyclist going right may try to shoot out in front of F. If he has not stopped – beware!

Motor cyclist G might try to pass F, skid on the wet patch E and slither towards D, ending up in "your road". Your glances will have included H, warned by arrow M, the beginning of a double white line and I, a double bend sign. *Don't let your gaze dwell in any one place.*

Frightening? Yes, but not if you abide by the golden rule:

DO NOT DRIVE AT A SPEED FROM WHICH YOU CAN'T STOP IN THE PREVAILING ROAD CON-

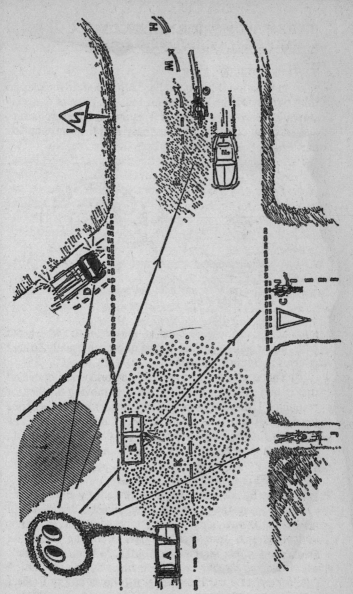

Fig. 33. Flashing the eyes.

DITIONS, WITHIN THE DISTANCE YOU CAN SEE IS CLEAR (OR IS GOING TO BE CLEAR).

TWO "EXPERTS" TIPS.

(a) In situations like that in fig. 33 the good driver keeps a thumb ready on the horn ring. A toot can prevent danger – stop a jay walker for example. This preparedness saves half a second and often life! It is less easy with the centre button

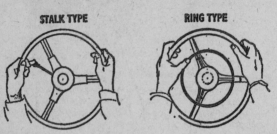

Fig. 34. At the ready for the horn but with the hands still in full control of the wheel.

horn push because your hand is needed on the wheel, but with ring or stalk type horn push a finger can usually be kept ready. Fig. 34 shows you this.

(b) The expert will also "cover" the brake and clutch so that in any emergency no time is lost in moving the feet for stopping. The feet hover over the pedals *without pressing them*. Speed will be in check anyway but if it gets too low the right foot can occasionally give a dab of acceleration, returning to the "cover" position while danger lasts.

MORE REFINED ROAD READING.

Examine fig. 35. Apart from checking for walkers like H who may leave the pavement thoughtlessly, driver A will glance at the oncoming vehicles, especially E. E may, not noticing your L plate, decide to pass D, forcing you to use your 5 feet *safety margin K* or brake. Watching his front wheels *without dwelling on them*, is one way you can antici- pate for unless a car is skidding, it follows its front wheel direction.

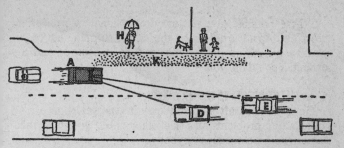

Fig. 35. More refined eye – flashing.

PEDESTRIAN CROSSINGS
Right of way. Gradualness the secret. Stop! Children Crossing Patrols.

Zebra crossings are illustrated in the Highway Code. Road side beacons flash orange day and night to warn you.

RIGHT OF WAY

Pedestrians have right of way and *you must give way*. The rules on whether to stop or not are clear. The pedestrian has the right of way *on the crossing* and if you hit him or drive where he is about to walk, *you are at fault*.

If people are standing on the pavement you don't have to stop. But you should be wary.

If any have stepped onto the crossing but are waiting, you stop unless too sudden a stop risks a pile up from behind. On test you would normally stop.

If there was ever a danger, e.g. someone rushing out with no possibility of *avoiding them*, you *must*, of course, EMERGENCY STOP TO SAFEGUARD LIFE, even at risk of a hit from behind.

Train your eyes to look at both pavements on approach and the central reservation if one exists. If anyone is crossing you must stop, or slow sufficiently, using speed judgement and commonsense, so that he has passed *before* you get there. Where there is a centre reserve each side should be treated as a separate crossing.

When you have had to stop and the last walker has crossed far enough for you to continue, you go, but not so soon as to frighten him.

Where possible give a slow down signal at pedestrian crossings. As a learner err on the side of stopping but never wave a pedestrian on for that can be dangerous and an examiner could fail you.

GRADUALNESS THE SECRET.

Good drivers only stop suddenly in emergency, as a rule anticipating problems and slackening speed gradually thus saving sudden stops for everybody.

Know the zebras in your area, because they are sudden stop hazards. I recently saw a pile up of five cars in daylight on dry road. The first stopped beautifully in emergency; the other idiots had been following too close.

STOP! CHILDREN CROSSING PATROLS.

When you see one of these men or women be prepared. When they step out displaying the sign you must stop. Apply the same care as for a zebra. Where policemen do this job they use hand signals as in the Highway Code. Be sure you understand police signals and obey them.

GIVING WAY AND YOUR "SUPPOSED" RIGHTS

If being overtaken. Obstructions. Passing parked cars. Passing cyclists. Meat in a sandwich. Lane discipline. Narrow "humped back" bridges.

IF BEING OVERTAKEN.

An overtaking vehicle, though he shouldn't, may have to cut in front of you. *Don't accelerate – let him in*, slow down if necessary. A few madmen accelerate and *cause head-on, death accidents*, killing innocent and guilty.

Don't accelerate when being passed. You could become involved in the accident.

Remember:

DO NOT DRIVE AT A SPEED FROM WHICH YOU CAN'T STOP, IN THE PREVAILING ROAD CONDITIONS, WITHIN THE DISTANCE YOU CAN SEE IS CLEAR, OR IS GOING TO BE CLEAR.

I am repeating myself but I want to get this message over. For all I know you may be pretty dumb!

When being passed, normally keep a steady speed taking care neither to close the space in front into which the overtaker intends to go, nor to slow so that the overtaking car could not drop back, if a fast approaching car forced him to do so. Be alert. If danger looms ahead and you see the man alongside braking to fall back, don't you brake and leave him in jeopardy. Rather you would accelerate to provide safety margin. Commonsense!

As far as possible let ambulances, fire engines and police cars pass when you hear their warnings. In thick traffic, if they approach *on your side*, try to move in and wait. Occasionally you can wait at green lights while they cross or turn on red.

OBSTRUCTIONS.

If passing any obstacle on your side and there is not room because of approaching traffic you *must give way. A rule of the road.* Try always to give way to anyone approaching uphill.

You slow and if necessary wait till you can pass safely and return to "your road" *without any approaching vehicle having to decelerate, brake or, worse, take avoiding action.* The test is, will the oncomer have to slow? If so, or if doubtful, *give way.*

In fig. 36 U has to stop for the approaching cars A and B. Should a fool or cad, passing a parked car on his side, make

Fig. 36. Giving way at road works.

you brake, don't accelerate or swing out in anger – as too many do. *Slow up.* Two dead cads do not make a gentleman.

PASSING PARKED CARS.

In fig. 37 you are A and need to move out to pass parked car D. Mirror watching shows car B close behind. You think B wants to pass. He may not have yet seen D if your car hides his view.

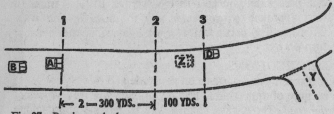

Fig. 37. Passing parked cars.

Imagine your speed is 35 m.p.h. Because of B you give a brief right signal till your mirror shows B realises why. Cancel it, or if a hand signal, withdraw it by point 2 (or you may find yourself like the car in fig. 38!) You make it brief to prevent misunderstanding especially as there is a turn at Y. If no cars behind, no need to signal.

From point 1 begin easing out gradually so that by 2 you are ready to pass D. *Learners often move out too late* and get stuck behind at 3 unable to see round and being passed and hooted. Ease out early, gradually and never suddenly.

Positioned correctly, at 2 you can see round D and decide whether you have time or will have to stop at Z. Always drop speed by 2 ready for stopping at Z if need. Between 1 and 2, you take 3rd or if need, 2nd.

The decision at 2, whether you will have to wait at Z, depends on conditions but you must stop on your own side and *back* enough – usually 25 to 40 feet – from D to see ahead. At 35 m.p.h. point I would be 300 to 400 yards from the parked car. Early positioning is vital and warns followers and oncomers. If the parked vehicle is occupied glance at his front wheels to confirm he will not pull out; also beware of the driver or passenger opening a door.

See fig. 38. If your flasher has not returned, cancel it. Others may try to tell you by a toot or a headlight flash from behind but the warning light inside the car tells you as well.

Fig. 38. If your flasher has failed to return to normal by itself, cancel it! Here, someone might think you were going to turn into the driveway or the lane.

PASSING CYCLISTS.

Leave cyclists extra room (5 feet plus) even if it means slowing and tagging *well behind* for several hundred yards before you can pass. Cyclists can wobble or fall off. If you reach an obstruction or are about to turn left at the same time as a cyclist you usually let him go first.

MEAT IN A SANDWICH.

You are A in fig. 39. There seems room to pass the parked vehicles without crossing the centre line but E is coming fast,

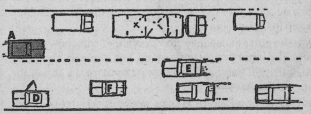

Fig. 39. Meat in a sandwich.

overtaking the other traffic. Should you? You know what happens to meat in a sandwich, so take no risk.

In similar situations never go on where you might be endangered. Car E could be forced out by F. Car F may not have seen E in his mirror, or may have to move out if D opens his door. A pedestrian might walk out from between the parked vehicles on your side or a driver open his door.

Slow in advance of the sandwich situation and wait, if necessary, till E has gone. Car E is at fault for trying to pass when you are coming; but if you were over the centre line I fear you would be too.

Remember our advice about the three-quarter mile view for if such situations are pre-judged and speed judgement used a full stop may be avoided. In slow traffic such passing is often safe. You watch parked cars for moving off or doors opening. Where there is room leave sufficient gap for this not to matter, but not to the extent of getting on the wrong side of the road if a car is coming. A toot may be necessary but empty cars don't move!

Be sure no children are around who may run out. Always flash eyes under vans etc. to check for walkers.

LANE DISCIPLINE.

Double queues often form, especially near traffic lights or roundabouts, and there are accepted customs.

(a) The inner lane may move quicker than the outer with overtaking on the inside. *This is allowable where there are definite queues,* but don't "cut" from one queue to the other in order to jump traffic.

(b) The inner queue may meet an obstacle such as a parked car. You must GIVE WAY to the outer queue, until there is a gap for you to join it.

(c) The outer queue may stop because of someone turning right. The inner one now flows on and those in the outer wait, either till the right turner clears or there is a gap in the inner queue.

(d) Cyclists and motor cyclists weave in and out of crawling traffic streams and you are best to yield as far as reasonable. This involves good mirror watching and, at first, advice from an alert teacher.

(e) For going straight on you may keep in either queue unless white road surface arrows direct otherwise but for turning right or left move to the appropriate queue as early as you can.

AT NO TIME, on catching up a single car that is "hogging" the road centre, may you pass it on the inside, *unless it is turning right*. You *must* follow till it moves in or you can pass on the offside (right) safely. You might hoot or flash your lights to warn him of your presence.

NARROW "HUMP-BACK" BRIDGES.

At blind "single file" hump-backs be wary. Some fool might shoot over from the other direction. *Slow down*, hoot when near enough to be heard, *proceed carefully*, in to your own side and ready to brake.

Until you see over the brow watch for the *instant the roof of an approaching vehicle appears* ready to brake and hoot again at that second.

One of you must give way. I know of no ruling but courtesy. As a learner give way. Remember the "I was there first" shouting match is idiotic, but whoever is nearest the top would probably go first.

OVERTAKING

The secret. Get back to safety. The warning hoot. Three "overtaking" Questions. Overtaking on three lane –two way–roads. Avoid the sandwich pass. Room for me too?

THE SECRET.

The secret of overtaking is staying *well back* enabling you to watch far in front of the vehicle to be passed. You move out towards the road centre a fraction for the best view but pull back for traffic going by the other way. Where the road curves to the left you may see ahead by looking through to the *left* of the vehicle you intend to pass.

When clear, and assuming you know no-one following is about to pass you, move out for the overtake, gradually, never sharply, at the same time maximising acceleration and confirming all is safe. The Highway Code urges you to signal (with right winker) prior to moving out. If dangerous drop back to where you were before and can watch for another opportunity. VISION and "timing" is the message.

In fig. 40 you are doing 40 m.p.h. ready to overtake the van and he 25 m.p.h. You are pictured having begun the gradual moving out process with your acceleration well under way. Space Y to your left is available to drop back into should a fast car approach. You can see well beyond the van if there is time and room to pass and return to your side.

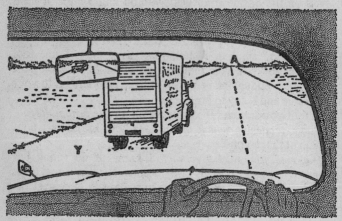

Fig. 40. Overtaking.

Being on strong acceleration while you moved into the position shown in fig. 40 will have given you several m.p.h. "in hand" for passing safely. Your teacher will at first have to tell you if you have enough speed to go on from here but experience will soon tell you what extra acceleration will now be available. Generally, to be sure maximum acceleration *will be available*, if you are to overtake a vehicle doing less than 40 m.p.h. *you must use a low gear*, changing up again afterwards.

(a) Starting to overtake from below 20 m.p.h. this will be 2nd.

(b) From speeds below 40 m.p.h., 3rd. In three gear cars use 2nd if below 35 m.p.h.

From your fig. 40 position things can still go wrong although the road looks clear; the van driver may swing out if his concentration lapses – unusual yes, but it happens; or, there might be a cyclist or child running out on his inside, unseen by you. So as your eyes scan ahead for danger, also flash them to his front wheels. If they don't turn out, he won't hit you. *Give a warning hoot before passing*. Allow 4 or 5 ft. between you and him while overtaking.

GET BACK TO SAFETY.

You need plenty speed "in hand" to pass quickly and return to your own side, so exposing yourself to danger for the shortest time. It is suicidal to pass with only a couple of m.p.h. "in hand" because it takes so long during which unexpected disasters may occur. Passing lorries needs more time, more acceleration and superior judgement of pace.

Never normally "cut in" after passing but return to your side promptly. *Do not stay on the wrong side just because it is clear. Get back*! A quick glance in your centre mirror or better over your left shoulder tells you how soon you are clear to come in but at first your teacher must guide you verbally. Check that your winker has cancelled.

If you have almost passed someone and an approaching car worries you *when it is too late to drop back*, give a left flasher to warn the vehicle being passed that you are being forced to move in and to show the approacher that you are getting out of his way.

THE WARNING HOOT WHEN OVERTAKING.

Don't hoot too soon, only when you can be heard but *still have time to drop back*. I stress this as many drivers swing out on hearing you – "thou shall not pass" types or possibly drivers who seeing danger ahead hope to warn you.

On wide roads horns are rarely needed in passing, when you have plenty of room to your right, but glance at those front wheels and always hoot weaving types and learners.

If passing two vehicles, *always* hoot the one nearest you.

THREE "OVERTAKING" QUESTIONS.
Question 1.
Is there a *gap ahead* for me? In fig. 40 the van is not close

behind nose to tail traffic and it is therefore safe. To overtake in traffic, without a gap is criminally dangerous.
Question 2.

Even at the "point of no return" can I still brake in behind the van if necessary? For safe passing allow for the worst. Is it safe if a road-hog comes at you from A in fig. 40 at 120 m.p.h.? Don't chance it if not and find yourself forced to cut in perhaps causing an accident.

Check that the driver following you is not moving to block your safety margin Y, fig. 40. Many evil or stupid drivers do. If you see him beginning to fill that space, unless you are sure all is clear ahead, better to slow and drop back allowing the fool to pass you.
Question 3.

Are *none* of the "DO NOT OVERTAKE" rules in the Highway Code going to be broken? Never try to pass in this world by risking passing into the next.

OVERTAKING ON THREE LANE – TWO WAY – ROADS.

Traffic is usually fast and it is dangerous if overtaking drivers incorrectly use the middle lane or stay in it unnecessarily.

The custom for overtaking on three lane roads is to *give way* to any approaching car *already in the middle lane* even if it is far off. Decisions, of course, depend on distance and the speed of your traffic stream and his.

In fig. 41 K is contemplating passing J, but A is already *in the middle lane* half a mile distant.

If K, you might imagine, "I will be safe to move to the middle lane and pass because A can drop into the gap between C and D before I get there." *Don't do it*. Let A come on. He may wish to keep in the overtaking lane to pass D and E and F, especially if the road is clear behind you.

Here's why. Firstly courtesy, but more importantly: the stream ahead has no long gap for you to drop into; the only way to get in would be to "force the issue" which could leave you in danger if one of the drivers was nasty; C might close on D and leave A similarly caught.

Result, disaster, because you and A would need to brake

Fig. 41. Three lane roads.

hard and there might be no time for you both to stop without crashing or the fierce braking might throw your car into the oncoming B, C, D. There might be a car Z following close on A, *but unseen by you* till A had filled the gap C – D, possibly too late. A might stick to his rights and keep coming. Any of the cars in either direction might swerve at the wrong moment jeopardizing the paths of either A, Z or your car K.

AVOID THE SANDWICH PASS.

By using speed judgement avoid the situation in fig. 42.

W is passing X and is sandwiched for a second while Y goes the other way – this is deadly because the slightest miscalculation by anyone can be disastrous as could a mechanical fault, burst tyre etc.

Fig. 42. The sandwich pass.

If caught in a situation like the above in *possible*, though not actual danger, choose the lesser risk. Thus W would stay nearer X than Y because hitting X would be safer than a head-on. Y should keep closer to his edge than to W. This is defensive driving the importance of which is scarcely realized yet. If more cars are close behind Y, your risk is greatly increased, as any one may pull out.

ROOM FOR ME TOO?

Never overtake a vehicle which is about to move out to overtake. Never pull out when about to be overtaken.

Don't pass blindly following a driver overtaking in the hope there will be room for you both to return to your own side. Often there will not be. If the front driver was forced to brake to get back behind the car you would almost certainly crash.

THE DISAPPEARING GAP.

Never overtake where a car in front of the one you wish to pass seems likely to slow down thus robbing you of your gap and possibly exposing you to death.

Part Three

Tackling The Many Kinds Of Road Junction

TURNING LEFT

Whose right of way? Turning left off a major road at a T junction. Left turn at stop sign onto a major road. Looking right and left. Left turn at give way sign onto a major road. Positioning for left turns. Positioning leaving a minor road to go left. Positioning leaving a major road. Turning left at cross-roads onto a major road. Left turns off the major road at crossroads. Don't overtake others who are turning left.

WHOSE RIGHT OF WAY.

At junctions it is usually obvious which is the major road. The minor one having broken lines across where it meets the major and a GIVE WAY sign near its end, or solid lines and a STOP sign.

TURNING LEFT OFF A MAJOR ROAD AT A T JUNCTION.

Fig. 43 imagines you are going to turn left *off* your (major) road. At A in fig. 43 you are doing 35 m.p.h. some 250 yards from the turn and the road ahead is clear. The side road is empty.

At A you reduce acceleration and at B, about 175 yards from the turn, take 3rd gear. By C_1 braking if need, you should be down to a running pace when you take 2nd. You can now turn at walking pace, slipping the clutch if need but *not allowing the car to freewheel* (NEVER do this – examiners rightly mark it against you), and re-accelerate in 2nd until C_2 before taking 3rd and so on. C_1 and C_2 are about 30 yards from the turn.

In slowing for the turn aim to make any braking you need

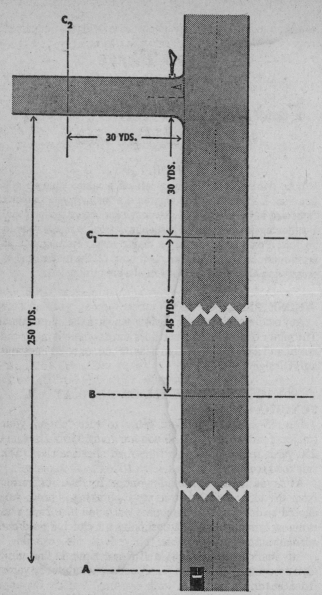

Fig. 43. Making a left turn off a major road at a T junction.

almost imperceptible. Only with practice will your judgement of pace achieve the smooth ride this allows. Leaving it late – and having to brake fiercely is bad.

LEFT TURN AT A STOP SIGN ONTO A MAJOR ROAD.

This time you are on the side road, fig. 43, about to turn left into the major road.

If the sign says STOP, you *must stop completely*, no matter whether all is clear or what a driver in front did, were there one. Failure to stop equals test failure.

Imagine the distances A, B and C. from the turn in fig. 43, applied to the side road. You take 3rd as before at B, but need not go down to 2nd. You brake, while in 3rd and stop *when the front of the car reaches the line*. Particularly watch out for pedestrians during last few yards. To prevent stalling, clutch down during the last few yards. Once stopped, apply the handbrake and slip to neutral before releasing the foot-brake or clutch.

You stop at the line, not "miles" before, so as to see both ways along the main road. If, after stopping, you can't see, edge forward till you can, but watch your car nose is not chopped off.

When the road is clear right and left take 1st and go, accelerating to normal speed without dithering. A "killer" to watch for is *two* cars, one overtaking the other, *coming from the left*. STOP OR DIE!

LOOKING RIGHT AND LEFT.

The common instruction at junctions is *look right, left and right again and, if safe, proceed*. But rules are for fools, more is needed. (One-ways deceive followers of above rule.)

In fig. 44 the car driver followed the rule at A but crashed at C. The steep camber (see page 47) caused him to take longer than he expected to reach C let alone D. He knew the lorry was coming quickly but thought he had time. *Never* think it is safe – *know it is safe*.

(1) Follow the look right, left and right again rule – but keep instantaneously eye switching right, left and *ahead* to where danger may lurk *while crossing*. Had the driver in fig. 44 done so he could have stopped at B.

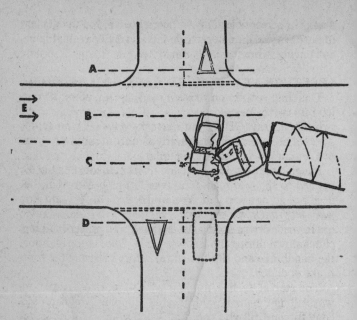

Fig. 44. "Feeding her" when crossing danger areas.

(2) Had he moved more smartly he would have reached D safely.

The message is: *get your accelerator going before, as, and after you let the clutch up, to be sure to get you over the danger area, safely, quickly.* If you don't you might stall and be hit. Never linger.

(3) The lorry driver in fig. 44 should have anticipated the car might stall and slowed – *ready to stop.* He was Part II of the accident. Had he been observant he might have guessed from the car driver's face that he would pull out.

Many drivers don't slow sufficiently on sight of a car starting to cross ahead. They rush on thinking they can stop which they can't.

LEFT TURN AT A GIVE WAY SIGN ONTO A MAJOR ROAD.

See fig. 43 again. If you are turning left from the side road and the sign says GIVE WAY, you do take 2nd for the last 20 or 30 yards before your turn. Here's why. You don't have to stop completely if all is clear. Being in 2nd and at slow speed, you are *prepared to stop or go*.

If the road-end and the major road are open, eye flashing to the right and left (and if a cross roads, ahead) beforehand enables you to decide what to do. If there is any traffic on the major road then, as instructed by the sign, you GIVE WAY. Stop at the end. After, you can proceed as for a STOP sign, meantime remembering handbrake on and into neutral. But if no traffic is on it you can turn without a complete stop taking care and with eyes ranging. Keep slow so that if a car appears you can easily GIVE WAY at the last moment. Were you not to and caused the car to brake or alarmed the driver your test pass would be in doubt. This is "his" road.

POSITIONING FOR LEFT TURNS.

For these turns – left from major into minor and left from minor into major roads, positioning is vital. Memorize my message. CORRECT POSITIONING AT ALL TIMES PROBABLY PREVENTS MORE ACCIDENTS THAN BRAKING, ESPECIALLY KILLER ACCIDENTS.

POSITIONING LEAVING A MINOR ROAD TO GO LEFT.

From before you take 3rd approaching a major road to turn left you begin to ease to your side. By the turn your wheels should not be over *two feet* from the side. Swinging wide during the turn is a fault.

Fig. 45 shows two incorrect "lines" through a left turn and the correct one:

(1) Wrong, the turn too wide all the time.

(2) Wrong. The car swung out to clear the pavement. It didn't need to.

(3) Correct.

There are more reasons for taking line (3). If you have to stop at the end of the minor road, a following driver or cyclist going right can come alongside you unhindered. By your position, traffic knows that you are going left even if you forget to signal, or if your signal is obscured.

Cyclists and motor cyclists should not be able to squeeze between you and the pavement but check by glancing over

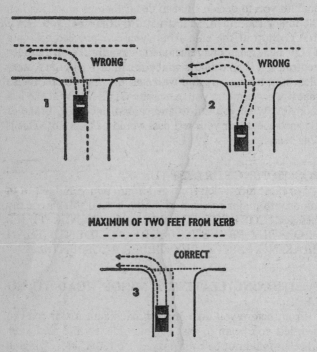

Fig. 45. Positioning during left turns.

your left shoulder through the side and back windows. If there is a cyclist, stop and let him through or make sure he stops or you would crush him on the turn. *Cyclists shouldn't do it but do.* If you have to wait at the junction check before moving. The reason for keeping about 2 ft. out is because people can step off the pavement and to avoid the kerb. Commonsense.

POSITIONING LEAVING THE MAJOR ROAD.

Approaching your left turn off a major road hold a steady course well to the left and watch for cyclists. *Do use* slip roads if provided; thousands don't seem to know they should. By taking the correct line, following motorists can pass safely, earlier.

TURNING LEFT AT CROSSROADS ONTO A MAJOR ROAD.

The rules for a T junction apply but as well as eye flashing to right and left include glances ahead. If you were B in fig. 46, waiting to go left (not across as shown) and there was a

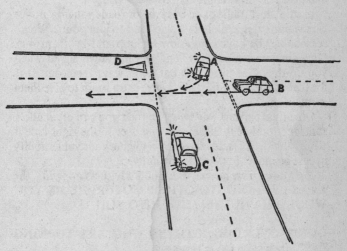

Fig. 46. A crossroads problem.

car at D, waiting to turn right and no car A, would you go in front of him or wait? You can often go while he can't move because of traffic like C, but if he starts his right turn before you move, *you must wait*. It is dangerous to cause him to stop in the middle of a major road.

If a car at D was coming straight across, your left turn would be unaffected.

LEFT TURNS OFF THE MAJOR ROAD AT CROSS-ROADS.

Fig. 46 shows a common hazard. You are C on the major road positioned to turn left, travelling slowly and within 15 to 20 yards of your turn. Assume for the moment there is no car at A, then B, because you are turning left, thinks he can nip across in front and does so.

Or perhaps there is a right-turner waiting, like A shown, and he sees you are going left and thinks "I can shoot over".

Let them go if they start. Reason? It would be more hazardous for them to get stuck in the middle, therefore for the safety of all, give way. Because a driver is selfish, is no reason for having an accident. Guilt is usually hard to prove and losses of "No-claims" bonuses are costly.

In stop-start traffic or on busy major roads you may notice cars waiting desperately in a side road to join yours. Where reasonable, be courteous, slow or stop and let them out. Give ample warning by a hand slowing-down signal when you do this. (See page 104) but don't wave them out. It is for them to decide if it is safe. Leave extra room to give them extra vision.

On a dual carriageway two lane road you can often allow someone to filter in left by moving over to the right lane if clear behind. This adds safety by reducing your vulnerability in case he moves forward accidentally.

Keep away from danger is as good advice as applying the golden rule DO UNTO OTHER MOTORISTS AS YOU WOULD HAVE THEM DO UNTO YOU.

DON'T OVERTAKE OTHERS WHO ARE TURNING LEFT.

Remember the Highway Code rule *Do not overtake* at, or approaching, a road junction. This applies to *all junctions*, even insignificant ones. In practice, if 100% safe, experienced drivers overtake left turners as they slow but only when THEY can see in all directions that no one could be endangered. If unsafe, THEY HOLD BACK. As a learner don't pass near a junction.

TURNING RIGHT

Procedure leaving a minor road. Positioning to turn right onto a major road. At the turn when the law says stop. At the turn when the law says give way. A positional "catch" turning right onto a major road. Method for right turns off a major road. Hidden dangers turning right. Right turns at crossroads. Turning right from the minor road at crossroads. Turning right off a major road at crossroads.

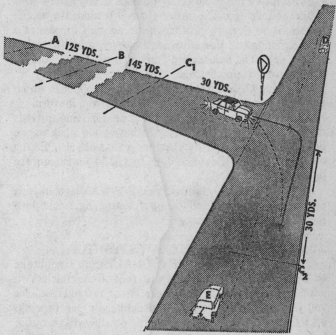

Fig. 47. A right turn.

PROCEDURE LEAVING A MINOR ROAD.

Fig. 47 helps to illustrate. Approaching the minor road end you slow, braking where necessary and drop down the gears as for turning left. See page 85. If you are going to stop, as in fig. 47, no need for 2nd gear as you will go to neutral when stopped, but where there is no stop or halt sign take 2nd *ready to stop, or to turn and get away.*

POSITIONING TO TURN RIGHT ONTO A MAJOR ROAD.

I have not advised you to check the mirror before positioning, as *I have urged the need for continuous mirror checking. You should "instinctively" know what is behind by now.* However, on test, it is wise to make a deliberate check before positioning, preferably moving the head slightly as this lets the examiner see you are making correct mirror use.

Begin positioning earlier – perhaps 300 yards – even sooner if followed. The closer a car is behind, the sooner you begin to ease over, otherwise it may try to pass at a "wrong" moment. For a learner, however, it is often wiser to slow and let a "bull-necked" driver pass so giving yourself a less nervewracking passage.

Study fig. 47. From A reduce speed, dropping to about 25 m.p.h. before taking 3rd at B, 175 yards from the turn.

Also at A, about 300 yards back, begin moving towards the crown of the road, aiming to have your right wheels just inside the centre, by the time you reach C_1. Easing out is gradual and should be done by C_1, 30 yards from the turn.

At C_1, take 2nd only if there is a GIVE WAY sign and it is possible you may not need to stop; for stopping, retain third then neutral when stopped.

AT THE TURN WHEN THE LAW SAYS STOP.

You *must* stop for a STOP OR HALT sign. Handbrake on and neutral before allowing your foot off the clutch. You *must take neutral.* Reason? Your attention *might* wander and you could relax pressure on the clutch or your foot slip off it, resulting in jumping forward, possibly disastrously. Let the clutch up once out of gear, as holding it down for long wears it.

The handbrake must be on to prevent rolling forward or back. It is easy to slip back and hit the car behind unwittingly!

Once stopped, check with eye flashing *both ways* because there might be a fast driver like D in fig. 47 or worse, one *overtaking* the other. When clear don't cut the turn, see dotted line fig. 47. Follow the arrowed path, adding speed to get you away quickly, safely. Conditions permitting you would be up to third gear by C_2.

Study fig. 47 again. Take 1st just before moving off. If D were the only car, you would take 1st as or shortly before he passed, *ready to go as he cleared and before someone else came up.*

Don't dither, give the engine plenty of revs.

AT THE TURN WHEN THE LAW SAYS GIVE WAY.

At a GIVE WAY or SLOW sign if you see in advance the major road is clear, go on without fuss. If you have to *stop* proceed as for a STOP sign.

A POSITIONAL "CATCH" TURNING RIGHT ONTO A MAJOR ROAD.

As you position for this there can be a catch. Look at fig. 47. Car E may do a fast wide left hander, or car D a tight right hander and swing across "your road". *The latter is common, be prepared.* You may have to brake or swerve in. But, a driver following, preparing to go left, may have come up inside. (Correct positioning allows him to as you may have to wait longer than he). If you can't move in, you have to stop.

It's better to *anticipate*. If such a situation is likely don't pull out so far. You may perhaps hold up the following driver but prevent an accident. Use your eyes, anticipate, THINK.

METHOD FOR RIGHT TURNS OFF A MAJOR ROAD.

Study fig. 48. Ease out gradually beginning 350 yards or more from the turn to a position just left of the road centre by C_1 250 yards from it. Brake if necessary, and change down.

You must be in 2nd by H (40 yards from the turn), speed reduced and in *complete mastery of the car*. Positioning, slowing and taking 2nd, you watch approaching traffic to see if a *stop* is needed. If there is a safe gap on arriving at the turn make it confidently; in 2nd you have the power to get safely round. As you did not have to stop, the risk of stalling is less. If in doubt, stop.

Your early flashers, positioning and brake-lights warn

followers to be ready to stop or slip through on your left, if there is room.

Take an example. Study fig. 48. You may be unable between C_1 and H, or even after H, to judge if you will arrive in time to turn before A is too near. A is continuing on the major road. You are to turn off it. Therefore, it is

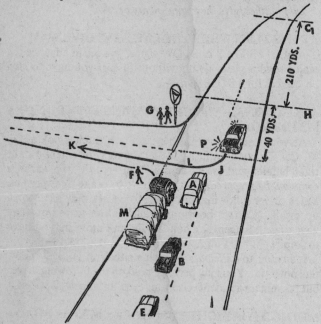

Fig. 48.   A right turn off a major road.

your job to GIVE WAY (if need) by waiting. Of course, A may decide he will stop to let you through. Correctly in 2nd you are ready to get quickly out of danger, to K.

When you have to stop do so with the front of the car on an imaginary line which is a continuation of the centre line of the minor road as fig. 48. Handbrake and neutral for all inclines or if waiting more than seconds.

Then, *anticipating* the next safe gap for turning take 1st shortly before the last approaching vehicle passes. Give firm acceleration before, as and after you release the clutch to be certain the car will take you safely out of danger.

Lay two lengths of string or tape parallel a road's width apart for 70 yards or more. These represent kerbsides. Practise pulling in to the "kerb" forwards and backwards. You aim consistently to be able to stop parallel to and a foot from the kerb (or less). Practise mainly for the passenger's side of the car next to the kerb. Your side is easier and less important. Learn to reverse in a straight line (no wandering) by backing along your "road" at a set distance from either kerb or in the centre.

Place cartons about 18" wider apart than your car as shown. Practise driving, slowly, between them. As your gap judgment improves you will be able to go quicker. Reduce the gap and test your skill.

3 *Place boxes 18" wider than your car. Now approach the gap from an angle. For practise keep tightening the angle till it becomes almost impossible. See how good you can get! First forward, then in reverse.*

4 *Drive up to a box till the bumper almost touches it but doesn't. Do this forwards and backwards till you know the length of your bonnet and boot. When good at the exercises pictured think up more yourself.*

5

An exercise to help later with the three point turn. Learner is checking how far from the tape or string the bumper was when she stopped. Practise stopping about a foot from the string.

6 *The same exercise as above in reverse. Look out of the back window over your left shoulder with a glance or two over your right shoulder as an extra check. (Don't open the door to lean out.)*

7

Details of how to do a three point turn are in Part 1. Photos 7–12 give the main points in sequence. This shows the car pulled in correctly a foot or less from the kerb.

8

The steering is put into full lock immediately the car moves, within 2 or 3 feet.

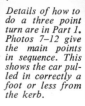

9

Keep this initial (right hand) full lock on as shown here till the last 3 or 4 feet from the opposite kerb.

10

During that last 3 or 4 feet put the steering into the other (left) lock. Here is the car stopped about a foot from the kerb, now with the steering in full left lock or nearly so, ready to reverse back.

11

As with the forward move, keep on the turning lock till 3 or 4 feet off the kerb. This photo was taken just before changing back to the right hand lock for the final forward move. Our driver here has left it to the final possible moment.!

12 ▶

Here she is stopped a foot off the kerb already back on to full right hand lock, prepared to go forward.

13

The "hover cover" position is explained under **Road Reading – Two "Experts" Tips** in Part II. The feet are at the ready over the brake particularly, but also the clutch, without touching them.

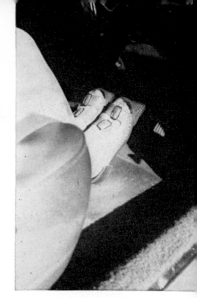

14 *Shows the danger of children running out from behind a badly parked car. Our driver had anticipated and was able to stop.*

15 *The car had hidden the child. Our driver was in control having seen feet underneath the car earlier. Watch under stationary vehicles.*

16 *The driver of the car from which this picture was taken is attempting to pass dangerously. The car had stopped to let children cross* **...**

17 *Where NOT to park! Such parking forces others to break the double white line rule. Study the Highway Code for list of prohibited parking places.*

18 *A situation you will often see. Your road is clear but traffic in the other direction queues. Watch, because jay walkers may run from between stopped traffic. Keep speed down and drive well away from the queue. The white car, who had plenty of room to his left but didn't use it, found himself having to brake sharply for this pedestrian.*

19 *Never block your back window like this or have your mirror askew. Give other such cars a wide berth.*

20 *Where there is street lighting you assume a limit of 30 m.p.h. Here there are repeater signs showing an exception to the rule. If there is lighting but no limit, repeater signs tell you.*

21 *A badly worn tyre photographed in a car park. At least a third of all accidents involve skidding, of which bald tyres are a major cause. Our roads* **are wet** *about 30 per cent of the year and it requires 2½ times the stopping distance using a bald tyre like this.*

22 *This picture was taken with an electrically operated camera from a car travelling at 60 m.p.h. on a skid-pan. As explained in our section on aquaplaning a water wedge has built up between the tyre and the road so the tyre has absolutely no contact with the road. Although the car is travelling at 60 m.p.h. the front wheel is stationary and the car is out of control.*

23 The first picture ever taken of a car aquaplaning at just over 60 m.p.h. on a wet surface. The rear tyres with good modern design treads are revolving and driving the car, but the smooth front tyres have no contact with the road surface and are motionless as shown by the white painted ¼ section and the hub cap. A smooth tyre is incapable of moving the water from under its contact area with the road, and water builds up in front of the tyre.

24 *This car doing 60 m.p.h. was fitted with Dunlop SP.41 radial ply tyres. The tread pattern is displacing the water to the rear so that the tyre remains in contact with the road. The tread pattern is gripping the road even at 60 m.p.h. where a worn tyre would not.*

25 *How to park between cars. Photos 25 to 29 show the correct steps in sequence. This shows pulling up ready to begin. Question 26 in Part IV gives you full instructions. A good idea is to practise first on an open space using cartons as cars and string to represent the kerb.*

26 *Reversing in with full left hand lock.*

◀

27

The moment to change to right hand lock.

28 ▶

Here you are almost "in" but not yet straight. One forward and another backward move during which you straighten up should get you parked correctly as in the next photo.

◀

29

Having straightened up be sure the car is in the middle of the space before leaving. Then if the car ahead or behind need room to manoeuvre, they have it.

30 *This narrow bridge makes it impossible to get through except in the middle and therefore you must wait to let an approacher through unless he waits for you. The correct position to pull up if waiting, is shown.*

31 *Never sit at lights straddling the two lanes. Here, I was unable to move forward ready to turn left as a result of the waiting driver's bad positioning.*

Wait for a gap long enough for you to cross at a mile-an-hour. You go faster but *need that safety margin*. I regret repetition but the killer is stalling. Use *resolute*, not ferocious, acceleration.

The line, (long arrow), is the same whether you stop or not. You start turning only from when the nose of your car passes that imaginary line (dotted in fig. 48), *not before*. Don't cut through P.

In fig. 48 I show the stopping position waiting for cars A, B and E to pass. Don't creep while waiting for E. Some drivers creep to J which is wrong as it prevents a clean turn.

HIDDEN DANGERS TURNING RIGHT.

Pedestrians G and F in fig. 48 could prove awkward if they crossed as you started turning. You dare not hit them and could have to stop at L. Due to the lorry parked wrongly at M (see Highway Code), cars like E could not see you were to be forced to wait and might hit you. The moral is be sure your path is clear before beginning the turn.

Another hidden danger in fig. 48. When stopped awaiting a gap *never* start turning the steering. If you did and some ass, without noticing you had stopped, hit you from behind you would be shunted round into any oncomers. KEEP THE WHEELS STRAIGHT TILL TURNING. Remember this "no turning till started" rule, especially on fast roads where you are the only stopped car. While waiting watch for motor cyclists appearing on your right – let them go first.

RIGHT TURNS AT CROSSROADS.

You imagine a centre point to the crossroads and go round it. Never cut across. This is the rule.

Study fig. 49. Your path is shown by the solid arrows and those of cars A and B by dotted ones.

TURNING RIGHT FROM THE MINOR ROAD AT CROSSROADS.

Unless the crossroads are *clear* in *all* directions, always stop. At STOP or HALT signs you must, but do so at GIVE WAY and SLOW signs too. You can then concentrate on checking for all clear. Your positioning and slow approach are as for turning right on to a major road at a T junction. Having stopped, be patient till the major road is clear both ways, (in fig. 49 from both H and I). If a car stops for you, you must still check for danger from all other directions and for scooters etc. from behind that car.

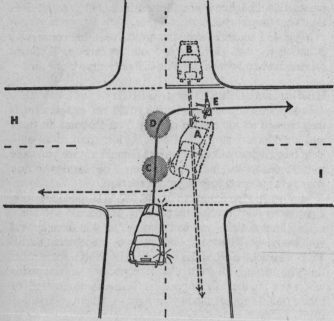

Fig. 49. Turning right on to a major road at a crossroads.

When H and I are clear the chief risk is from traffic from opposite. As you wait watch if they wish to turn right, left or come across.

With H – I clear, if a car opposite is waiting, you can go, but it often happens while you are deciding to move he does too so that you both set off at once. Don't panic. Slow traffic stops easily. If this happens and he is turning right, you both go round the imaginary centre point and each other. If he is going across you still go round the centre "point" after he clears. That is the theory. You stick to it but beware if he cuts in front. Be ready to stop at C if he does. Fig. 49 shows this going round each other. Doing this it's important you check for hidden dangers such as the motor bike E, behind A.

From D, if there is no more traffic from opposite, you go smartly on, following the solid arrow. If there is other traffic be ready to wait at D if any pulls out. No one should – *anyone ought to wait like car B in fig. 49*, but often people are naughty and if someone pulled out you would then have to go round behind. If a car opposite pulls out to turn to its left, you tail in behind.

Wherever possible avoid such waiting at C or D as has been described for real danger exists from fast traffic from H or I. I have told you what to do if you get stuck only because there will be times when you have to stop unexpectedly.

The danger is from fast drivers not realizing you are *stuck* in the middle. They kid themselves you will be clear before they arrive, delaying braking till the last second, perhaps too late! Such fools often hoot rudely, believing that they have right of way which, in law, they may not have.

But, if you shot out, knowing a car was coming and hoping to get clear but had to stop at D, causing that car to brake, the driver would have reason for anger and it could mean test failure.

TURNING RIGHT OFF A MAJOR ROAD AT CROSS-ROADS.

Position and slow as for a right turn off a major road at a T junction, see from page 96.

You wait for a gap in the approaching traffic and go round the imaginary centre point. Any crossing traffic theoretically waits till you clear. If it doesn't, stop and use your commonsense to clear as soon as safe.

GOING STRAIGHT AHEAD
When on a major road. At crossroads if you are on the minor road. A quick glance and away is not good enough. Which queue?

WHEN ON A MAJOR ROAD.

At all turnings but particularly at crossroads, be alert. People *often* pull out carelessly. Either they don't look, look and don't see, foot slips off clutch or they drink and drive.

Although on the major road, always slow down in readiness for a chance of trouble.

Much depends on the road width, approaching traffic and how much you can see of the side road, on the degree of danger if someone pulls out, on the space available for avoiding action and on how quickly you know you could stop. A hoot should warn a driver of your presence if you think he has not seen you.

A junction swarming with pedestrians is different to one with none, so make allowances.

There are no rules but here are suggestions. Approaching a small crossroads on a wide country road with good vision all round, slow to say 35 m.p.h., slower if you "smell" trouble. Picking up speed again is easy. The hard thing is stopping for danger for which be prepared *always*.

A different story is the approach on a narrower road to a crossroad with vision limited by woods, hedges etc., you may have to drop to 10 or 15 m.p.h. or less to be safe. A hoot can often prevent trouble, but go slowly, never rely on the horn. For very narrow *"blind"* crossroads, town or country, walking pace and stopping may be imperative.

Driving on a major road does not license you to kill. Your duty is to avoid accidents and the examiner will note your care, or lack of it.

AT CROSSROADS IF YOU ARE ON THE MINOR ROAD.

If you intend to go straight on, even if the sign says GIVE WAY, it is better to stop and confirm all is safe.

A QUICK GLANCE AND AWAY IS NOT GOOD ENOUGH.

One glance may not be enough to reveal all. Cars may be hidden by the blindspots of your windscreen pillars, your passenger's head, dirt on the windows, or on your glasses etc. A second look picks out any moving vehicle hidden previously.

Thorough eye-ranging is essential. Thousands of smashes occur because people do not understand the danger of these blindspots.

WHICH QUEUE?

When a double queue forms at the end of a minor road, which queue for going straight across? The right is normally best, as it allows left traffic to filter away but stick to the queue you choose.

UNMARKED CROSSROADS

Beware. Watch out for other people. Headlight flashing.

Found mostly in town side streets and country lanes. The safe rule, whichever way you are going, *including straight across*, is to stop or practically so before going if safe.

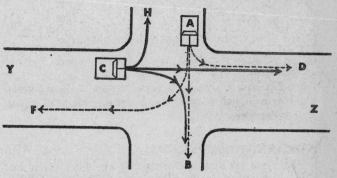

Fig. 50. An unmarked crossroads.

BEWARE.

In towns parked cars often line crossroads and hide them till too late. What can you do?

Be eagle eyed. Drop speed so low a stop can be instant. Hoot.

WATCH OUT FOR OTHER PEOPLE.

Fig. 50 shows a crossroad where Y–Z is probably the major one BUT you are not sure because there are no signs. You can come on them suddenly if inattentive and smashes are common because many assume "Oh! It's my right of way" and speed on regardless. Your rule? *Slow and* GIVE WAY *to all unless they stop for you.* Your examiner will be watching care.

Remember it is not your job to wave on other traffic and it can cause accidents.

In fig. 50, chances of fatal accidents between A and B or C and D are probably highest, next from A to F, or C to B. Accidents going from A to D or C to H are perhaps less likely to be serious. Avoid over-confidence.

Care at unmarked crossroads is one of the secrets of experienced drivers who have no accidents for years.

HEADLIGHT FLASHING.

Some drivers flash their headlights to indicate that you can go. Though well meant this may be confusing if cars are at all four roads. My advice is do not flash and be guided by what drivers do, not by their light flashes.

SIGNALS
When and how to signal. Flashers "system". Hand signals. Right hand signal. Slowing down signal. Left hand signal. Signals to police.

WHEN AND HOW TO SIGNAL.

I have not yet discussed signals, to avoid confusion. For all turns you need signals. Refresh your memory of *positioning*, speed and gear procedure at junctions, see pages 85 to 99 so that it is fixed in your mind. As methods for slowing and positioning nearing any junction are similar a signals "system" can be used.

You may be asked to use indicators at all turns for most of the test and hand signals alone for part of it.

Do realise a hand signal *alone*, is not always seen by cyclists or drivers like A and B in fig. 51. Cyclist A needs to beware of car C who (although very badly positioned) is signalling to turn left.

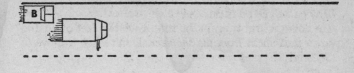

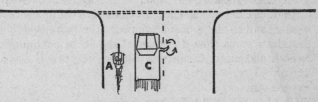

Fig. 51.   Where a hand signal is unseen.

FLASHERS "SYSTEM".

Start the flasher shortly *before* beginning easing into position for a right turn, or for turning left shortly before starting to slow down. Some exceptions to this, where a signal has to be carefully timed, I come to later.

Make sure it stays on, and that it has cancelled itself after the turn. At slight turns it often won't do this and within a short distance you need to cancel it by hand.

Remember to signal! Make it habit even if no-one is about or you may forget one vital time and endanger somone. Use left flasher when you intend to park at the kerb.

HAND SIGNALS.

Learn which hand signals you must know, what they mean, and what policeman's signals mean from the Highway Code. Master signalling and get your teacher to ensure yours are correct. Learners rarely give clear signals. Avoid the floppy nervous-looking signal.

RIGHT HAND SIGNAL.

Get three-quarters of your arm *straight* out with closed

fingers extended. Keep it at right angles to the car and horizontal. The palm should be sideways, facing the traffic.

SLOWING DOWN SIGNAL.

A straight arm is again the rule. Give two feet of up and down movement *from the shoulder*. Don't wave bye-bye to Granny!

LEFT HAND SIGNAL.

For clarity the left hand signal needs exaggeration. Give a forward circular movement (anti-clockwise) with the elbow bending rather like a crawl swimmer. The movements for this and for the slow down signal should be continuous, smooth and clear. Distinction between the two is everything.

SIGNALS TO POLICE from inside car.

The "ahead" signal is correctly done by pressing the whole palm of the hand on to the windscreen. For the left signal get your arm well forward to help the policeman see at once.

HAND SIGNALS "SYSTEM"

Timing right and left hand signals arriving at a major road. Timing right and left hand signals leaving a major road. The slow down signal. Signals when going straight on at cross. roads.

TIMING RIGHT AND LEFT HAND SIGNALS ARRIVING AT A MAJOR ROAD.

As mentioned you *must at all times* have AT LEAST ONE HAND ON THE WHEEL. Therefore bring in your arm during gear changing. Coming to a junction before turning right or left give the appropriate signal shortly before taking 3rd, hand back on the wheel as you change down then renew the signal, maintain it till roughly 30 yards from the turn or just before changing if you need 2nd.

Even if you are not dropping to 2nd you withdraw the signal, because at the turn you need both hands on the wheel and 100% concentration in case of emergencies.

If you stop at the end (for more than a second), repeat the

signal just before moving but if you don't stop (e.g. at a GIVE WAY) there is no need.

At police controlled crossroads, if stopped, you hand signal, maintaining it while you sit, to let the constable, and others, know your intention.

TIMING LEFT AND RIGHT HAND SIGNALS LEAVING A MAJOR ROAD.

Give your first hand signal shortly before beginning to position for right turns and for a left turn before beginning to slow down. As it is risky to give a hand sign over about 35 m.p.h. drop speed first. Withdraw the signal while changing to 3rd then repeat it till roughly 50 yards from the turn. For left turns off a major road, unless you stop, this signal in 3rd could be the last needed.

For turning right, if you have to stop in the middle of the major road to await a gap in the approaching traffic, give an extra signal (hold your arm out) while you wait till just before you go but bring it in for a moment if oncoming traffic is passing close.

THE SLOW DOWN SIGNAL.

You give a slow down signal to warn following traffic you are stopping *in the road*, or at the kerb, and that they *will probably have to stop* unless they can see they need not. It alerts oncomers, for example, at a zebra crossing. Practise them all the time and be ready for the test. For parking at the side this is the correct signal.

Some drivers say that you should alter a right or left signal to a slow down one if you can see you will have to stop and wait before turning. This is muddling because commonsense tells others if you are turning you may have to slow or stop, and your brake lights warn followers.

SIGNALS WHEN GOING STRAIGHT ON AT CROSSROADS ETC.

Generally if going ahead no signal is needed unless you require a slow one for such a reason as coming to a crossroads or traffic light where the driver behind was close and might not have seen the notice or lights. Particularly helpful

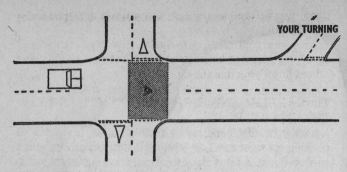

Fig. 52. When a late signal is correct.

is a slow signal if traffic is halting well back from the cross-road where the cause may be hidden to followers.

An exception to the no signals rule would be an ahead signal to police. Similarly the "palm-on-the-window" signal is useful if waiting at a traffic light with another man opposite who you think wants to turn right. At the light change he will know you are going straight across and he will have to go round behind you.

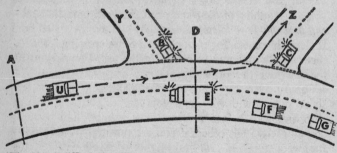

Fig. 53. A difficult signalling problem.

MORE DIFFICULT TURNING AND SIGNAL PROBLEMS

When a late signal is correct. Another need for a late signal. A vital tip. Positioning. Turning left and, almost immediately,

106

right. Turning right and, almost immediately left. Introducing a golden rule.

WHEN A LATE SIGNAL IS CORRECT.

In fig. 52 with the crossing shortly before your turn, to avoid confusion only begin to signal for it from area A, BUT, *slow down normally*.

ANOTHER NEED FOR A LATE SIGNAL.

In fig. 53 you are U. If going left at Z you should give a slow signal at A for those behind, next a brief left signal at D. This prevents B from thinking you are taking his road.

In practice, you could signal earlier because if positioned correctly (following the broken arrow) drivers B, C and E will know by *your "line"* and *speed*, you are going to Z.

The lorry E, in fig. 53, correctly positioned ready to go to Y, waits as shown until he is sure what U is doing and acts accordingly.

A VITAL TIP.

B, waiting to come out left watches U's front wheels, disregarding his flasher if it is on. Only if he saw those wheels turn and U starting to turn into his own road would he prepare to go. If you see someone flashing never trust his winker, watch his wheels; he may have forgotten to cancel it!

B would probably start as soon as U had passed, but must check that C doesn't decide he will now come out and turn right, or collision! However, C would probably delay with E only just clearing and F and G still coming.

POSITIONING.

Reflect on your line through this situation in fig. 53 (you are U) *and realise, "positioning", that is anticipation and getting into the correct part of the road, is, for safety, of greater importance than signals*.

I would rather drive a million miles with a driver who grasped the need for positioning, then ten miles with one who had disc brakes, safety belts, new tyres etc. but did not grasp this need.

Equally important is the correct adjustment of speed.

TURNING LEFT AND, ALMOST IMMEDIATELY, RIGHT.

In fig. 54 you are A, waiting to enter road B. D – E has dense, *slow* traffic. Notice two lanes on your side of it. You wait till both are clear and then move smartly. Following the arrow path to take up an immediate right turn "line," changing your flasher from left to right at G. You may have to wait at C for a gap in approaching traffic to make your turn.

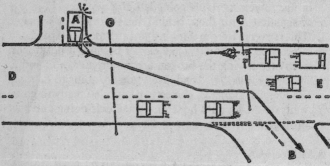

Fig. 54. Turning left and almost immediately right.

TURNING RIGHT AND, ALMOST IMMEDIATELY, LEFT.

This is similar but can be more difficult. You must wait for the road to clear *both ways* or for traffic to stop.

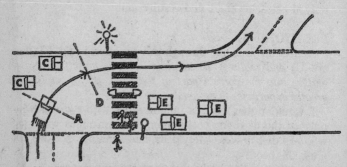

Fig. 55. Turning right and almost immediately left.

Fig. 55 is an example. Your line is shown by the arrow and from A you change your flasher to left.

Traffic E has stopped for pedestrians and traffic C has courteously stopped well before the zebra *deliberately* to let you move to D. Go to D only if both lanes C have *stopped* and traffic E is still held up by pedestrians, or, as it may do, is waiting for you. You wait at D if need for the walkers.

Experienced drivers give a courtesy nod a learner is not expected to give. If you do, *be sure not to sacrifice concentration and attention.*

Fig. 55 has shown how the courtesy of several can ease a difficult turn for one. Remember that lesson if you are ever able to help someone by waiting just a little longer. Normally driver A would need to wait for a long clear gap both ways.

INTRODUCING A GOLDEN RULE.

In fig. 56 U wants to go left into the main road. He must wait for a gap and be ready if there will soon be one. For example, D may slow or stop to let B turn, this allowing U

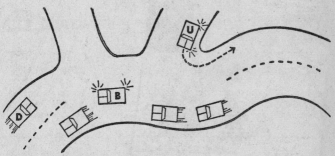

Fig. 56. A tip for turning left.

time to go smartly left. But there are pitfalls; D may still be going at speed (though appearing to have slowed for B) and have to brake as U would only be building up speed. U needs great care in this and *must wait* if in doubt whether D might be caused to brake. He dare not pull out hoping D won't need to brake and still less *knowing* he will need to. To do so would brake the golden rule below.

NEVER DRIVE INTO OR ACROSS ANYONE'S SAFE STOPPING DISTANCE.

This rule is a life saver so stick to it. The risk is you might stall in front of a driver who was daydreaming. On test even making someone have to slow can mean failure.

DUAL CARRIAGEWAY TURNS

The safe area for turners. Turning right onto the dual carriageway. Right turns off a dual carriageway. Left turns at dual carriageways. Don't make a mistake.

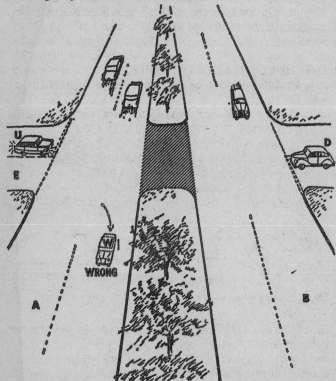

Fig. 57. Dual carriageway turns.

THE SAFE AREA FOR TURNERS.

The opening through the central reservation, shaded in fig. 57 is the "safe" area. It is here that, if need, you wait, "sheltered" from fast traffic.

TURNING RIGHT ONTO THE DUAL CARRIAGEWAY.

If U is turning right into dual road B in fig. 57, and dual A clears first, he nips over and waits on the left side of the space, (looking at it from E), prepared for his right turn. He may have to wait after B clears while D crosses to beside him (on his right) and if so, as normally, he then goes round, *behind D*, for his turn. He goes straight to the inner lane of B because of his slow speed.

D waits in the space, if dual A has by now got more traffic until it clears for him to go over.

If you arrive to turn right onto a dual road and find the reservation space full, wait till it clears or you may be "stranded" over a fast deadly road. If your road is wide wait near to the centre line to permit followers to filter left if safe.

RIGHT TURNS OFF A DUAL CARRIAGEWAY.

Fig. 58 shows a right turn *off* a dual carriageway. Wait in the forward half of the space leaving room for anyone wanting to turn right from the opposite direction; fig. 58 shows two cars correctly positioned. If the space is in use wait in the right (offside) lane, close to the edge, till it clears. Anticipate

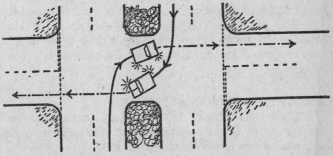

Fig. 58. Turns off dual carriageways.

this several hundred yards earlier and signal to forewarn followers.

LEFT TURNS AT DUAL CARRIAGEWAYS.

Left turns at dual carriageways need no further explanation. Apply normal rules and *care*.

DON'T MAKE A MISTAKE.

Extraordinary mistakes can happen, particularly at night. Fig. 57 shows one when U turns right. Not realising it is a dual carriageway he turns to W. You can imagine the result! If where you want to turn right onto a dual carriageway there is *no opening* through the centre reservation you *must go left*. Go along till you find an opening, position slow and signal, approaching it as if for turning right. Once positioned in the further half of the opening you should be able to turn fully right to go back the other way when safe.

TRAFFIC LIGHTS

Light sequences. The chief dangers at lights. Approaching lights. Waiting at lights. Danger from pedestrians if turning. Pedestrian "Cross" signs. Arrows on the road at lights. Signs at lights. Green filter arrows. A problem turning right. If red reappears before you get clear. Crossing in front when turning right. The light shooter. The two wheel queue jumper.

LIGHT SEQUENCES.

Study the colours in the Highway Code. Go to busy lights, stand and watch. Notice the sequence of the lights even if you *think* you know. You may find you were wrong! Watch what the drivers do and see which lights show in one direction compared to the other, count the seconds between changes.

THE CHIEF DANGERS AT LIGHTS.

Other drivers "shoot" the lights, that is, cross when the right is yours. Some pedestrians treat lights as crossings and wander over no matter which light is on.

Scooters and bikes weave in and out of slow traffic and

pop up at the wrong moment where they can be crushed. They may try to squeeze by on your left as you turn left.

Green changes to amber and you have to stop quickly. Always be ready to act.

APPROACHING LIGHTS.

Positioning, slowing, signalling and selecting the right gear at lights are similar to the procedures at crossroads. At

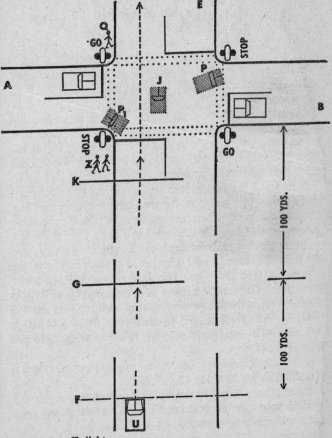

Fig. 59. A traffic light.

113

lights each road takes precedence in turn as the lights go green. At red each road, as it were, loses priority and by law, traffic must stop.

Make a few adjustments to your approach system.

Imagine in car U in fig 59 you intend to go straight on. Long before the lights your long-range eye flashing will have told you what colour they are likely to be when you reach them.

When possible you drive accordingly. For instance, if the light *changed to green* when you were 200 yards away at fig. 59 F, you would expect they would stay green till you passed. With little traffic and a clear road as in fig. 59 where the dotted arrow shows your unobstructed way through the lights, no need to drop below say 25 m.p.h. Judge how fast is safe allowing for road width and your stopping ability were a pedestrian such as Q to step in your path. Take 3rd at F to give you acceleration "in hand" if needed.

Alternatively, if you expected the light to be amber and then red before you reached it, you prepare to stop. Take 3rd as before, then down to 2nd by G, 100 yards before the lights. You are thus ready should the light remain green, for going through smartly in 2nd.

A frequent learner fault is not changing to lower gear, ready for snappy acceleration when circumstances demand. They labour in 4th when they ought to be in 2nd for pulling power; use this gear if low speed demands it.

It is correct to *continue on amber* if there is *no time to stop* but never go through red. If amber appears around (fig. 59) K take the lesser risk – going or stopping – judging by traffic conditions. You should already be in the correct gear if rapid acceleration is the better course. It is undisciplined driving (your examiner will know) to land yourself in a situation resulting in an emergency stop for red. The solution to this light problem is:

(a) reduce approach speed sufficiently to meet all events if you think amber likely and

(b) weigh up the possibilities well in advance.

Have your mind prepared and the right reaction will *come quicker if or when you need it.*

WAITING AT LIGHTS.

Waiting at red, handbrake on and out of gear staying in neutral till amber appears; on amber take 1st, but don't go till green and you are sure no-one is still crossing on amber (or red!) At green you give way to any pedestrian still crossing before going. As at crossroads, never wait in gear, or holding the clutch down.

DANGER FROM PEDESTRIANS IF TURNING.

Pedestrians like Z in fig. 59, don't usually cross when green gives you the ahead, as the light facing them is red; but, they cross roads A and B in the picture, as traffic on them will be stopped at red with green showing equally for the pedestrians as for you. This means if fig. 59 U wants to right or left he will be going as it were through the red of road A or B. If there are pedestrians he must give way and therefore he waits at P, (P_1 if turning left) but moves on, "against" the light, when the way is clear.

In turning right he may first have to wait at J before going round "through traffic" from E and should not move to P unless there is *no* traffic coming on road E, however if it is clear and he has moved to P but has had to wait there some time, traffic may arrive from E and be blocked. This can't be helped. But he must not deliberately edge in front of such traffic knowing that as he can't go through it will be blocked, rather must he not leave J till the walkers have crossed.

PEDESTRIAN "CROSS" SIGNS.

Some lights have "cross" signs for pedestrians who are thus protected, (your light shows red as theirs shows "cross"). Only when they are told to "wait" would your light show green. Where these signs operate for both directions, *all* traffic stops as pedestrians cross.

ARROWS ON THE ROAD AT LIGHTS.

As in fig. 60 enormous arrows sometimes show which lane to be in. Knowing the road enables you to take the correct lane early but it's easy to be "on the arrows" before knowing they exist.

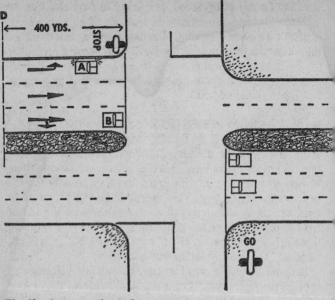

Fig. 60. Arrows on the road.

Don't panic or swerve if wrong; from what you know of positioning you should be in a reasonable place for your intended path and drivers around should be careful on seeing your L plates. Check mirrors, and over your shoulder(s) gradually correcting your position if you can. Unless there is time and a gap to correct your mistake you may need to abandon your intended turn. This is better than holding up angry following traffic.

Learners often leave lane positioning too late, arriving at red in the wrong queue. Signal and ease into correct lane about 400 yards beforehand. Put yourself in car B in fig. 60 and assume you intend to go straight on. If not already in lane at D, allowing for traffic behind and perhaps beside you (in addition to mirror work, take a glance over your shoulder) ease to the middle or right lane immediately you safely can. You are correct in either lane as each has an ahead arrow. Positioned early concentration can then be

116

directed on adjusting speed, preparing to stop etc., for the lights.

Note: To show D on fig. 60 I had to put it at the edge. It should be not less than 400 yards from the turn.

Fig. 61. Common signs at lights.

If in car A in fig. 60 going left, keep to the nearside left lane. With our appalling roads and increasing traffic, lane discipline is vital.

SIGNS AT LIGHTS.

Fig. 61 shows some common ones. They are found at many junctions as well as lights at which they are often fixed to the traffic light pole. No examiner will trick you into disobeying one but particularly remember the No Entry sign which has no writing on it.

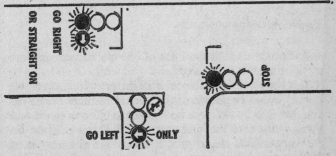

Fig. 62. A green filter arrow.

117

GREEN FILTER ARROWS.

These allow traffic in one lane to go while red stops others, or a separate filter allows them elsewhere. They can apply to left, right and sometimes ahead traffic.

If a green filter suddenly shows your lane can go, *go* where it points, *even if you have made a mistake in choosing the lane and don't want to!* You must not hold up correctly positioned followers! Fig. 62 is an example of what to do at a green filter.

A PROBLEM TURNING RIGHT.

I have shown this in fig. 63 at a non-traffic-light turn but it is frequently found at lights. Alas for an L driver like U in fig. 63, a junction is often busy; when a gap should come traffic has built up. Don't panic. If a cad hoots as you wait keep calm. *A hoot only hurts if you let it.* The position in fig. 63 is probably not dangerous as you are shielded by the

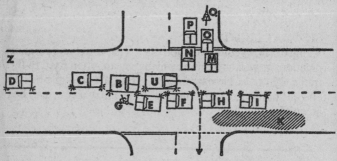

Fig. 63. A problem turning right.

halted traffic. U is at the front of one queue, waiting close to the centre line to turn right.

This is an extreme instance; if all drivers were fools a policeman would be needed or they would be there all day. In practice, E, F and G close up bumper to bumper and H and I wait a little back leaving a gap for U,B, C and D to use. So the congestion is cleared and E, F and G, who have been waiting, make their right turns when traffic from Z has ceased, followed by H and I. Then M, N, O, P and Q are clear to cross if no more traffic arrives along the main road.

A Catch in fig. 63.

U, before taking the gap left him by H and I, dare not go without checking area K as must each of those who follow. He edges forward till he can see round H. To shoot through could endanger a cyclist.

You could meet a situation like this where a verbal battle develops. A learner should keep silent. Normally the "weight of opinion" forces the fools to yield and be civilised.

At lights it is easier. In some congested areas, an adjustment allows several right turners through after other traffic stops before renewing priority for either direction but at most courtesy suffices.

IF RED RE-APPEARS BEFORE YOU GET CLEAR.

At a light a turning chance may not offer till after the light is amber (from green). There is then usually time (see fig. 63 again imagining there were lights), for U, B, G, E and F to take 1st and turn.

C, only just beyond the light stop line, would wait or if space behind could drop back as could H and I. M and N would probably wait for this to happen.

It's all commonsense, laced with self-preservation.

At lights it would be bad luck if a speed merchant either shot off on amber (+ red) or was so discourteous as not to give an L driver time. If it happens, stop, wait, and let the experienced drivers circumnavigate you till the position opens. You may later need to back up or try going on or get your teacher to guide you. *Remember you can wait.* Every red light has a green lining!

CROSSING IN FRONT WHEN TURNING RIGHT.

Normally, at crossroads, where two cars turn right from opposite directions, they go round each other. At a few lights there is an exception to this rule. Crossings exist where, by custom, often due to the weight of traffic in one direction or to the layout of the roads, vehicles, instead of going round each other, pass in front. (Left side to left side). It is less common, but happens, where there aren't lights.

Fig. 64 shows a light controlled crossroad. Both turning cars must go carefully around the shaded area, lest traffic which may be hidden springs from the points D, to which *they must give way*. Crossing traffic in fig. 64 is halted by the red light.

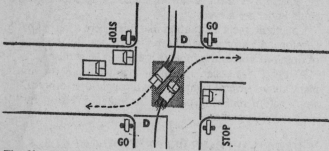

Fig. 64.   Crossing in front when turning right.

At a crossroad imagine going straight on on a MAIN road and an approaching vehicle risks turning right just ahead and across you. *Danger?* You brake enough to just miss the idiot car not realizing motor bike(s) or smaller cars hidden from you behind that vehicle may commit themselves to swing across you as well, *leaving little chance to miss smashing into them.* BE SLOW ENOUGH to allow for this unseen risk till you see if it exists.

THE LIGHT SHOOTER.

Even when green shows for you there are drivers who, intentionally or in error, shoot across you on red. It happens often but particularly on wet Saturday nights. Your eagle eyes alone can save you because the "enemy" is generally speeding. *Train your eyes to spot these maniacs coming.* Expect danger where a crossing is blind because of buildings etc. Light shooters are one of your greatest risks.

THE TWO WHEEL QUEUE JUMPER.

One expects cyclists to weave ahead in queues but watch for them when turning left or right as some of them seem to take no notice of danger. Glance over your shoulder be-

120

fore moving at green and normally *give way to them*. These pests are found near lights, but can be dangerous anywhere.

POLICEMEN ON POINT DUTY
Traffic wardens.

POLICEMEN.

Learn the meaning of *their* signals and the correct ones to *give them* from the Highway Code. They pop up controlling traffic at all kinds of places. Do as you are told, stop – or go *if safe* – remember even policemen make mistakes though rarely.

Turning right you would go "round" the constable unless he directed you in front; he would give an obvious sign. Position normally and take the usual care with other traffic, pedestrians etc.

TRAFFIC WARDENS.

Traffic wardens help directing traffic in some areas. Obey their signals which are the same as those of police.

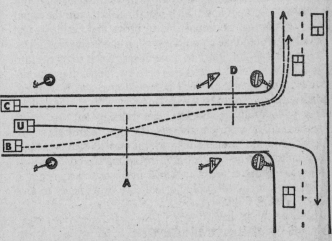

Fig. 65. A one-way street.

MERGING.

One-ways traffic tends to move faster and crowd the left side but it's probably safer – no "head-ons". Normally, keep as straight a route as you can. Your problem starts when you want to turn or ease right or left. Begin to move to the side you want, twice as early as usual, signalling well in advance because people keep to lanes, even if none are marked. Avoid speeding, one-ways are not race tracks. You can overtake on the left provided you watch the driver you are passing does not want to merge left.

In fig. 65 you are U and want to turn right. Your path is arrowed. What happens at A will depend on the action of B who is going left. C has few worries before his left turn until point D where his and B's path merge.

By custom at merging points A and D the driver already "in lane" has his way and the man who wants to merge waits. Courtesy, *never force*, works wonders. At A (since you are both merging, though in opposite ways), as your car nose (U) is in front of B, he should let you go *but don't count on it*. Use commonsense and if he looks like cutting ahead avoid a "battle". Scrapes and higher insurance rates are the usual result. Guilt may be impossible to prove and besides a test examiner would take a poor view of an aggressive candidate.

At D, car C should try to make it easy for B to merge into his lane. He might accelerate, or slow, depending on circumstances, but keeps alert. B should give way if worried. The exception would be a wide one-way with a wide exit on to a wide road where two lanes turning left (or right) simultaneously were possible side by side. Were this so, B, in fig. 65 would not need to work his way to the inner lane, moving to it, if he wanted, after rounding the corner.

At the end of a one-way which meets a two-way in a T junction as in fig. 65 apply normal care being ready to give way or stop.

MORE DIFFICULT MERGING.

Car U in fig. 66 has to cross the one-way street to B. He

awaits a gap to enter, then, using his left flasher would as opportunity arose, with use of the mirrors and care but more important – by glances over the left shoulder, make his way to the left lane ready to enter road B.

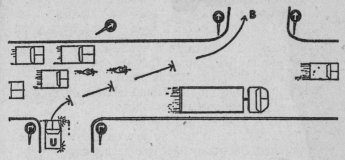

Fig. 66. Difficult merging in a one-way street.

The line should be more or less direct as arrowed but in traffic the operation might have to be stop-go as breaks in the arrow show. It depends on how many lanes of traffic are flowing, their speed and how easily one can merge over. Practise to gain confidence for the test.

Try to avoid others having to brake suddenly or you could fail for not being careful.

AN L DRIVER'S NIGHTMARE?

Look at fig. 67. Not really a nightmare, but study such an area on foot or as a passenger to gain insight. Arriving later at such a situation without being mentally prepared could be worrying.

Few serious accidents occur at such busy one-way junctions. U must watch *his* traffic light B and not, say, D, because it activates the crossing traffic from H which can cross to F or turn to G or J or K. Moving on the wrong lights you could cause an accident. It happens easily, so be alert.

Were U going to K in fig. 67 he ought to have taken the position of M beforehand, but, though wrongly positioned, he should manage to ease with care, to the correct lane by about C_1 as the area is wide and little traffic follows him.

123

Approaching roundabouts. Signals at roundabouts. Left at the first exit. Other exits. Once on the roundabout. Spotlight on difficulties. "Round the block" roundabouts.

APPROACHING ROUNDABOUTS.

Roundabouts are clockwise one-way systems devised to reduce speed and make traffic flow safely. Here are some methods of using roundabouts. They are not firm rules but commonsense smooths unusual problems.

While approaching the roundabout take 3rd or 2nd gear as required and position the car as follows:

1.) For the first exit left, in the left lane

2.) For an exit that is more straight on than it is to the right, in either the left or right lane having regard to the weight of traffic approaching with you, or on the roundabout. The Ministry advise using the left lane where possible. I

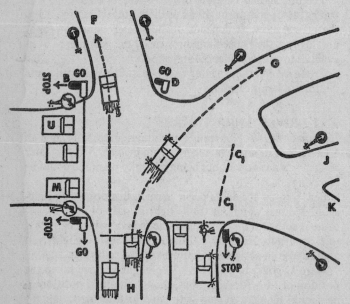

Fig. 67. An L driver's nightmare?

consider this advice foolish but include it as the Ministry have issued it.

3.) For an exit that is more to the right than it is straight on, in the right lane.

You frequently need 2nd gear to prepare you for stopping or going.

Some roundabouts have "Give Way" signs on the approach roads and dotted lines across the end of each road at the entrance, some only the dotted lines. At the entry to

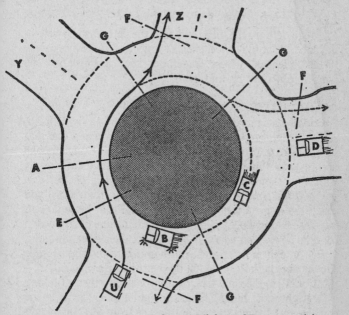

Fig. 68. A roundabout. See text for new Ministry of Transport advice.

all roundabouts, however marked, *give way to all* traffic from your right.

To reach A car U in fig. 68 has to consider car B. Unless he can clear across B's route well ahead of him *in time*, so that B would not need to slow down, he must give way to B. If

U waits for B, he still cannot go without checking that C has begun his left flasher and is not going on round, or watching D who may have forgotten to signal. If U was making for Y it would be polite to wait for B, also making for it, even with plenty time.

SIGNALS AT ROUNDABOUTS.

On all except the widest roundabouts you only normally use flashers. To negotiate a roundabout both hands are needed on the wheel to steer round.

LEFT AT THE FIRST EXIT.

To go left at the first exit, set the left flasher well in advance. It should cancel itself as you leave, otherwise cancel it! Experienced drivers sometimes keep a finger on the flasher control to remind them.

OTHER EXITS.

For all exits more to the right than they are straight ahead, position right and flash right on approach; take a line that will "hug" the roundabout from E in fig. 68. To let someone across your "line", do not swerve to avoid them, simply wait. Hug the roundabout *till there is a straight line between you and the point F applicable to your exit*, that is, till you reach the appropriate point G, fig. 68. From G change to left flasher and begin taking that straight line BUT, watch for cars *already on your left* by a glance over your shoulder.

For an exit more straight on than it is to the right I have shown one method in fig. 68 by the solid arrow to exit Z, – positioning in the right lane on approach exactly as if taking a far right exit, but NOT using right flasher; leaving the roundabout having started left flasher from G. This would be the correct line if the right lane on approach was empty and the left lane full of traffic (not shown in fig. 68 to avoid confusion) flashing to go first left.

A second method for going to exit Z can be used if the right hand lane on approach is full and is equally correct but needs care. Keeping to the left lane on approach, you enter the roundabout when a gap is free, and go round, *making a second lane round*, well to the left (or outside) of any traffic "hugging" the roundabout. Once past any exit to the left before your "straight on" exit, begin signalling left. You would normally give way to any traffic that has been hugging the roundabout that is also making for your road. This is why such traffic, as mentioned, should check for traffic already on its left by a glance over the shoulder.

If the exit road is wide enough this giving way may not be necessary as both of you could enter the exit road parallel to each other. Cars C and D in fig. 69 are about to do this but car C needs to be ready to fall behind if traffic from road 5 could be hampered. Car F in fig. 69 waits for car E which has been crossing from road 3 to 5 using the second, "outside lane", method described.

ONCE ON THE ROUNDABOUT.

You may have to stop to let someone entering fast in front of you (Many ignore the recommended "Give Way" advice) and at just a few roundabouts you are made to wait for *incoming* traffic by extra Give Way lines.

Should you mistakenly pass your breakaway point (G), go round again. *Never reverse.*

SPOTLIGHT ON DIFFICULTIES.

The chief faults at roundabouts are: 1. Not "hugging" the roundabout for far away exits. 2. Not entering and leaving in as "obvious" (positioned) a line as possible. The latter causes confusion and slows traffic flow.

Fig. 69 shows lane discipline. The vital thing is that *others know U wants road* 3. Cars X, Y and Z signalling to go left, keep left, while as U wants road 3, he positions onapproach in the right lane. For this difficult roundabout, although in effect going straight on, U flashes right, on approach, to avoid confusion.

Depending on his speed (fig. 69, A will be watching), U waits, before changing to his left flasher, till after his normal "flasher" point G. He delays at least till B to let A know he will not be taking A's road. He then flashes left. To judge when to change flashers put yourself in A's place. It's all commonsense.

"ROUND THE BLOCK" ROUNDABOUTS.

You may find huge one-way systems round buildings or whole blocks, in effect, vast roundabouts. Here you may have a good distance in which to ease from a right to a left lane, or to a lane marked for your route by a road arrow. Thanks to this distance, in seeking a gap to join the appropriate lane, it is often unnecessary to stop.

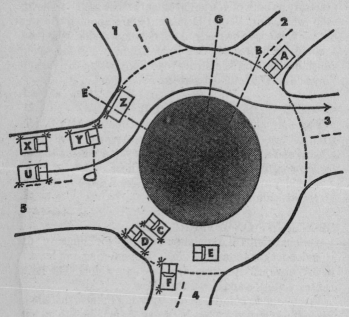

Fig. 69. A difficult roundabout.

With skill and speed judgement, after practice before the test, you usually find it possible to merge into your lane without inconveniencing others and well before your exit.

Provided you are faster than those in the lane you are joining (if the lane was empty speed would not matter) and are clear of them, merging into a lane is like overtaking. Don't "cut in" on the car you pass. If you are not sufficiently ahead, slow and merge later. Your flasher tells all of your intended merge, and remember, drivers expect these merges.

If you miss the required lane DON'T panic, slam on brakes or swerve. Keep CALM. It may be safe to stop smoothly. Check mirror. If not continue in the lane you are "stuck" in. If in a right lane go on round for another try – armed with prior knowledge of the problem. If a left lane you can take a left exit you don't want and somewhere along it turn round or take another turn that will lead back to the roundabout.

On test an examiner won't mind if you can't merge but could fail you for a stupid or panic action. Panic normally *proves* inexperience. Do get sufficient roundabout practice.

Where a one-way system runs several hundred yards along one side of a giant "roundabout" *provided you are already in the correct lane*, cancel your flasher by hand if it's on to prevent followers thinking you have forgotten it; re-set it if required nearing the end of the straight.

Remember to keep those eyes ranging, lest traffic in front has to suddenly stop. Avoid sudden stops or swerving without warning, except in emergency. Treat "Mini" roundabouts (about 4 yards diameter) normally. They allow extra traffic to flow, usually in "lanes". A round blue background notice with large white circulation arrows announces them.

MULTIPLE CROSSROADS
Attitudes. Examples of danger.
ATTITUDES.

At multiple crossings not controlled by police or lights, you need to be sharp eyed. In places like fig. 70, *unless you are 100% sure it is safe to go on*, don't risk it.

Road markings and signs normally tell which is the "major" road. Even if you are on the "major" road someone on another road might imagine his had priority or might be mistaken. In any event, if "his" road had no "give way" sign, or even if it had, his position could be strong. Too many drivers assume being on a "major" road automatically grants "I can bash you" rights. Courts could take a different view. Roads are "yours" only if clear.

Never exert supposed "rights" and be certain the other

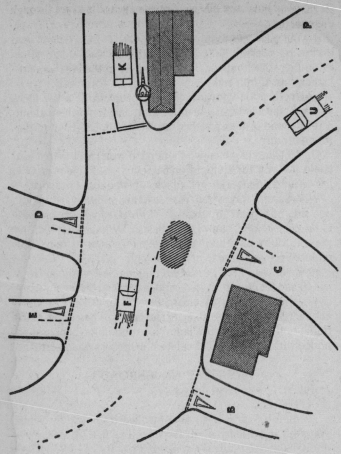

Fig. 70. A multiple crossroad.

man has stopped or will before going yourself. Flash your
eyes for everybody, ahead and to the sides.

EXAMPLES OF DANGER.

Study fig. 70. If driver U watch that vanman K doesn't
sail out not realising your road exists. Incredible, but it
happens. With the shops and being a van with poor side
vision his view is restricted. Beware of the van. That vans

are not allowed any side windows or even slits to see through should be sufficient to put all previous Ministers of Transport in jail for "murder". If these ministers had to drive vans the experience would so frighten them that the law would quickly be changed. *Your* vision is also restricted so slow lest someone appears.

K is danger man again if he mistakenly thinks F (who intends going down the main road) wants his road. Gaily speeding, stupid K comes face to face with F and *crash*! Beware of being K yourself. Clues to watch for, the curve on the centre line of the main road and the blind ending of the shop fronts on the left. Also the positioning and speed of F. But, to be like K you would almost certainly have failed to see the STOP sign – a test failing error.

If K wanted to go right to D, he would have to reach point J when safe, making a proper turn from there when clear. *He must not cut straight over and right.* If he wanted road E he would delay signalling till after J to make his intentions 100% clear.

Similarly were U going right he would signal normally for K's road but would wait for the correct moment to signal for D or E. The same applies if going left into C or B. All commonsense.

From fig. 70, B, to D needs an immediate left signal after your right turn as would going from D to B; also apply thorough eye ranging to be sure there is time to go over at a "mile-an-hour". To allow for the unexpected this long time is essential but actually cross smartly.

To go left from D down the major road you would signal left while waiting in D, cancelling it as you set off and steering straight down the major road towards P, so that anyone like K could not misinterpret your intention.

Part Four

Special Situations You May Meet – Questions – The Test

WEATHER

Fog. Fog in patches. Cloudbursts, torrential rain. Spitting rain.

FOG.

Deadly because too many forget the golden rule.

DO NOT DRIVE AT A SPEED FROM WHICH YOU CAN'T STOP, IN THE PREVAILING CONDITIONS, WITHIN THE DISTANCE YOU CAN SEE IS CLEAR.

As a learner, avoid thick fog. In a mist you could try but hand over to your co-driver if it thickens. Even experts find the strain of peering through the gloom exhausting after a few miles. It tires the eyes and only madmen continue when tired. Here are the main hazards and how to deal with them.

In fog *use headlights*. (most sidelights are useless). *Nearly as important as seeing is to be seen*.

Under "Night Driving" I explain the headlight positions.

In fog, *day or night*, use dipped beam. Full or "high" beam restricts vision rather than helps it. Use foglamps if you have them, as well as headlights, if possible.

Be sure your windscreen isn't steamed inside as this hinders vision. *Clean it and open windows* if necessary. In damp fog use windscreen wipers. Leaning out of your window may help you see better in extreme conditions.

Maximum fog speed may be *walking pace* or less. *Satisfy your conscience* your speed is safe. It takes *will power* not to be tempted to keep with the man who whizzes past. He may have superb eyes, or lights, or more likely, he is one of those born every minute. Beware of following a fast "fog" driver. What if he crashes?

Idiotic "following the lights" ends in countless pile-ups. Police should investigate all such disgraceful behaviour.

Often the only way in fog is to crawl near the edge using it as your guide. Range your eyes ahead, around – and up for traffic lights. Over concentrating on the edge could find you on a crossroads before your mind registers.

In towns street lighting helps but traffic makes driving correspondingly difficult. While advising on technique, I repeat, in dense fog, all learners and wise men stop. Why risk lives when you can sleep in the car or stay at a hotel?

FOG IN PATCHES.

It can be bewildering, especially at night, to run *suddenly* into unexpected fog. It is frightening at speed but unfortunately it is on fast roads through open country that patches are commonest.

Slow up at once – to a stop if necessary.

If you know patches exist drive slower particularly on a strange road.

With by now instinctive anticipation you will slacken speed to a safe level *before reaching any patch* and avoid danger. Don't speed on hoping to get through the patch quickly. Re-acceleration later is better than panic stations.

If surprised by a patch remember the man behind (he is in the mirror) and try not to jam on brakes but keep flashing brake lights.

CLOUDBURSTS, TORRENTIAL RAIN.

You should use dipped headlights day or night during the worst of such conditions, *to be seen*. Rain can be so blinding you have to stop. Choose a safe position, keeping sidelights on.

SPITTING RAIN.

Wipers used on a dry screen damage it. The first sweeps to clear initial rain, may stir up dirt and mask vision. Spray or splash from cars in front could increase trouble. Unnerving!

What to do.

(a) If need, *slow or stop at once*, keeping in to the left *till you can see again*.

(b) Use the windscreen washer to clear the dirt quickly.

(c) Or stop the wipers while rain water builds up so the screen is "washed" when you next switch on.

(d) *Be prepared* by having a clean windscreen to prevent the trouble.

(e) Look at the road, not the drops on the screen.

(f) Carry a clean rag to use if needed.

NIGHT DRIVING

Twilight or poor light. The headlight dipswitch. Which beam? Speed. Dazzling. In the country. In the town. More in the country. Reversing at night.

TWILIGHT OR POOR LIGHT.

Put on dipped lights. In teaming rain, fog, snowing, or generally poor *daytime* visibility, the *law requires* dipped headlights. A pair of fog lamps or one fog and one spot lamp may be used together with side lights as an alternative. It is illegal to drive in darkness without headlights on, unless there are street lamps 200 yards or less apart.

An advanced learner can practise at night even though the test is in daylight.

THE HEADLIGHT DIPSWITCH.

Ask your teacher to show you the dipswitch and the dashboard "High Beam" warning light. In some cars the dip button is on the floor as shown in fig. 71(D). Dipped lights shine near your edge of the road for a limited distance. On

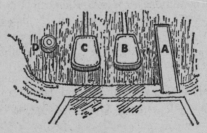

Fig. 71. The dipswitch. (floor type).

134

"High Beam" they penetrate their farthest. Practise working the switch while stationary and facing a wall.

WHICH BEAM?

Whenever there is someone ahead of you drive on dipped lights to prevent dazzling him by the reflection of your lights in his mirrors. If dazzled from behind yourself off-set your interior mirror a little to reduce dazzle but still enable you to see behind and try not to "fix" your eyes in the wing mirrors.

With nothing ahead of you High Beam is *essential to see properly* but can only be used when there is no oncoming traffic. *Whenever someone is coming – dip*, returning to High Beam immediately he has passed if no others appear. You can often prepare to dip in advance by seeing light beams approaching a corner.

For safe night driving you must learn proper use of your lights. Slower drivers often find traffic streams build up behind them at night and the many lazy (or perhaps fearful) ones who don't bother with High Beam but drive permanently dipped make overtaking them much harder. Safe opportunities are missed (because those behind are restricted in long range vision to the length of the slower driver's dipped beam) and resulting impatience often means hazardous risks are taken. Help those who want to pass by using High Beam. You dip once they are passed until they are well clear.

SPEED.

DO NOT DRIVE AT A SPEED FROM WHICH YOU CAN'T STOP, IN THE PREVAILING ROAD CONDITIONS, WITHIN THE DISTANCE YOUR LIGHTS SHOW CLEAR.

Speed MUST be related to the area lit. Speed on High Beam will be slower than in the day and on dipped considerably slower.

DAZZLING.

If you are dazzled (temporarily blinded) you *must* slow or stop till you can see. *Don't take risks or blame others;* you are responsible for your driving.

The inexperienced tend to be dazzled because they allow their eyes to dwell on or be "hypnotised" by the lights of the oncomer instead of looking where they are going.

Don't imagine that keeping clear of oncomers is enough. This is perilous because you become dazzled watching their lights, and in steering to keep clear you drive too close to them. Most serious, pedestrians, cyclists or obstructions on your side are not seen. Reduce dazzle by *concentrating on seeing your side of the road*, and keep your eyes *off* the approaching beams.

Many motorists go faster than is safe. DO NOT be tempted – luck ends. Driving within the limit of your ability and eyesight takes *will power*; show self-discipline by doing so.

If an approaching driver has forgotten to dip a *brief* up flash of your lights should remind him but of course to deliberately dazzle back would be stupid, only increasing danger.

IN THE COUNTRY.

Keep headlights on always. Don't be tempted, as many do, to use sidelights when following others. There are reasons. You will be less visible and your width may be wrongly identified. Vision is gravely reduced and the excuse that sidelights prevent dazzling the driver in front is irrelevant because if he is dazzled he should be going *slower*. Of course you can avoid dazzling him by dropping further behind. You might use sidelights only in a crawling traffic queue but headlights on when you move off. All common-sense.

IN THE TOWN.

In *towns*, dipped headlights *always* unless street lighting is super. Even if you see without them, it is vital you should be *seen*. People leaving sidestreets, take a quick look and pull out; they shouldn't, but they do. In their glance they miss tiny sidelights especially if their attention is momentarily diverted to a car *using headlights, further behind you*. Headlights also save pedestrians.

One day perhaps the law will be changed and larger sidelights or headlights that can be switched on at a reduced brilliance enforced.

MORE IN THE COUNTRY.

In *country* night driving normally use full beam but never approach a bend, junction, hump-back bridge or hill top without being *ready* to dip or you may dazzle oncomers.

Flashing lights up and down even *if there is no apparent approaching traffic* announces your presence at hazards. Do so and drive cautiously passing dangerous side road-ends or where your "major" road has a "minor" one crossing it. *In the seconds you are dipped you see approaching light beams easily. In the seconds you are on full beam others see you.*

Coming up a minor to a major road or turning off a major to a minor, dip while turning. Keep lights efficient, they are life savers. It is seriously dangerous to drive with one headlight or just a spotlight. Others might think you were a motor-bike till too late! When passing pedestrians or cyclists if followed, give a brief right hand flasher to alert those behind to move out or slow.

REVERSING AT NIGHT.

Don't reverse at night unless you must, when holding one or other flasher on helps you to see, as does flicking the brake lights with the pedal. A reversing light makes it easier still.

AUTOMATIC TRANSMISSION

Only the right foot. The selector lever. Kickdown. General hints and some pitfalls. Wet or greasy roads. A new automatic.

ONLY THE RIGHT FOOT.

To drive an automatic follow this vital rule. It is:
USE ONLY YOUR RIGHT FOOT, NEVER THE LEFT.

You use *only* the right foot for acceleration and for braking moving it from accelerator to brake as required.

THE SELECTOR LEVER.

With the majority of automatic gears there are five positions for the selector lever. They are *Park, Reverse, Neutral, Drive* and *Lock*.

Park. This provides a safety hold on the transmission preventing the car running away should the handbrake fail when parked. Don't engage it when moving.

Reverse. Delicate control can be achieved for manoeuvring. In reverse, handbrake off, the car can be held by the footbrake (right foot) and moved smoothly at a mile-an-hour simply by releasing pressure of the right foot on the brake. For increased reverse speed accelerate *gently*, as required, returning the right foot to the brake to stop. Use featherlight touch on the accelerator to prevent giving too much at once. In manoeuvring, the car can be held by the footbrake while the selector is moved from Drive to Reverse or vice versa.

Neutral. In *neutral* the gears are disengaged. For safety, on most makes, it is only possible to start the engine with the lever in *neutral* or in *park*, so the procedure, if the car stalls, is to pull on the handbrake, then move the lever to *neutral*, re-start the engine and re-select the required gear.

Drive. In *drive* gear changes *look after themselves*. When you select drive before moving off, the gearbox automatically engages 1st, as you accelerate it changes itself to 2nd directly the appropriate speed is reached and after that, to top. All you need to grasp is the correct procedure for moving off. Assume handbrake on, engine started with the selector in *Neutral*, and ready to begin, you:

(1) Apply the footbrake *using your right foot*.

(2) Move the selector lever to *Drive*, release handbrake.

(3) *Hold* the car with the footbrake, check that it is safe to move off.

(4) If safe change the right foot from brake to the accelerator and gently squeeze it till you build up the speed required. To slow you merely apply the breake as needed *using the right foot* the gears change down automatically.

Lock. This selector lever position enables you to override the automatic upward gear changes and keep in low gear to give engine braking on steep downhills, or, for overtaking, to prevent the gearbox changing to top before you want it to. There is usually an upper speed limit above which you should not try to engage *Lock*; cars vary on this so find out about yours. Faster cars may have two lock gear positions.

KICKDOWN.

You may need rapid acceleration for which an accelerator "kickdown" mechanism is provided. This operates only when the selector is in *drive* and can be used from rest or from any speed. It will only operate below the automatically governed maximum of 2nd gear. (Most automatics have three gears only.) "Kickdown" speed varies from car to car but in some is as high as 60 m.p.h.

On pressing the accelerator fully to the floor *and holding it there*, the gears change down. Depending on speed this will be to 1st or 2nd (if not already in 1st). The gearbox thereafter only changes up as the maximum in each gear is reached providing the quickest possible acceleration. Release the accelerator pressure at any time and the gears immediately change up, speed levelling off.

What I have said may not apply to all automatic cars so go into all this carefully with your teacher beforehand.

GENERAL HINTS AND SOME PITFALLS WITH AUTOMATICS.

For uphill starts use the normal procedure already explained for starting off.

For steep hills only (more than say 1 in 7), you may need to alter the procedure slightly and instead of holding the car on the footbrake at (3) page 138 keep the handbrake on. While you are checking that all is safe give *slight* acceleration till you feel the car straining to go. For (4) you release the handbrake, increase the acceleration and away!

Never allow your handbrake below 100% efficiency. In stop-start traffic it may not be vital (except for the test) to use the handbrake at each level stop unless stopped for a long period but I do recommend you use it *always* when stopped at traffic lights, stop signs, Give Way signs and pedestrian crossings. When stopped for more than a few seconds, move the selector to neutral to prevent the car trying to creep forward against the handbrake.

Those who change to driving with automatic transmission should keep constantly in mind two main points.

(1) Never use the left foot.

(2) Waiting in halted traffic with the selector in *drive*,

keep your right foot on the brake – DON'T "REV UP" on the accelerator or you jump forward. Frightening but easily done! Those who change back from automatic to ordinary gears must remember to put the clutch down when coming to rest, which after many miles not using the left foot at all is easily forgotten.

WET OR GREASY ROADS.

On skiddy surfaces avoid using "kickdown" or forceful acceleration whilst cornering. Otherwise this may happen: the gearbox may make an automatic change up (or down) and the slight jerk and temporary loss of power to the wheels that occurs may cause a skid.

A NEW AUTOMATIC.

I have discussed the most common form of automatic and your teacher must explain other types. A new advanced system has been developed for the smaller British Motor Corporation transverse engined front wheel drive range. It is all British and is so good I will give it special mention. By courtesy of British Leyland Corporation I drove with this transmission several thousand miles.

Instead of having one *lock* position on the selector there are four and these are equivalent to the 1st, 2nd, 3rd and top of an ordinary car. You therefore have four gears any of which you can hold, as well as an automatic *drive* position. You can thus drive either automatically or make clutchless gear changes just as you would in an ordinary car.

In traffic you can start and stop in any gear or in *Drive*. For the smoothest progress in stop-start traffic, engage 4th (top). The car starts relatively slowly but exceptionally smoothly each time. Once traffic is accelerating the selector lever can be slipped into *Drive* or dropped down a gear for a quicker speed pick up.

With this gearbox you can eliminate the hazard of unwanted changes mentioned under WET OR GREASY ROADS by holding the gear you need. This does not mean you can corner too fast! You still need care, great care.

I rate it the best automatic in the world.

SOME SIGNS

More signs. Herring bone lines. Double white lines. Road works.

You must seriously study the Highway Code.

Here are a few of the less common, more easily forgotten or vital ones in fig. 72.

Britain has gone sign mad. We have too largely followed or added to overseas patterns. I am certain, our excess of signs by diverting *attention* and causing over-familiarity, is increasing danger particularly *at night*. Not one in 10,000 remembers the meaning of all these signs, duplications and variations and many are incomprehensible without previous memorizing, with which few bother. One must be mentally robust to withstand this idiocy. The French, with their logic, are far ahead on signs.

MORE SIGNS.

Consider the signs in fig. 73 and memorize.

.DOUBLE BEND:

SERIES OF BENDS

: TWO-WAY TRAFFIC · CROSSES ONE-WAY ROAD

TWO WAY TRAFFIC AHEAD

NO RIGHT TURN

NO LEFT TURN

NO U TURN

NO STOPPING ·CLEARWAY·

TANK CROSSING

DUAL CARRIAGEWAY ENDS

· MINIMUM SPEED LIMIT ENDS

LEVEL CROSSING WITHOUT GATE

Fig. 72. Some signs.

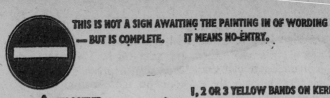

THIS IS NOT A SIGN AWAITING THE PAINTING IN OF WORDING — BUT IS COMPLETE. IT MEANS NO-ENTRY.

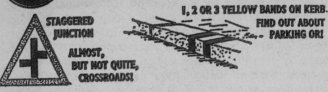

STAGGERED JUNCTION

ALMOST, BUT NOT QUITE, CROSSROADS!

1, 2 OR 3 YELLOW BANDS ON KERB. FIND OUT ABOUT PARKING OR!

YELLOW LINES AT EDGE OF STREET. DON'T PARK OR TROUBLE. FIND OUT WHAT YOU CAN OR CAN'T DO.

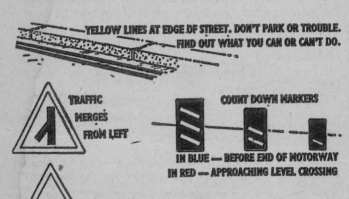

TRAFFIC MERGES FROM LEFT

COUNT DOWN MARKERS

IN BLUE — BEFORE END OF MOTORWAY
IN RED — APPROACHING LEVEL CROSSING

UNEVEN ROAD; IMPORTANT, SLOW UP OR IT CAN SCARE YOU

LOW FLYING AIRCRAFT   FRIGHTENING IF THE NOISE COMES LATER WHEN YOU HAVE FORGOTTEN ABOUT THE SIGN

MAXIMUM SPEED 25

MAXIMUM SAFE SPEED 25 M.P.H. A NEW EXPERIMENTAL ONE TO WARN THE MAXIMUM SPEED FOR THE BEND ON DRY ROADS

Fig. 73. More signs.

142

HERRING BONE LINES.

As fig. 74 shows a major road is sometimes marked by diagonal lines where there are turns off it. They form an elongated island which most drivers guess create a no-man's land. The lines round the edge have gaps so one *can* go on the diagonal area, which is intended to keep all out of the area *except* those turning right off the major road.

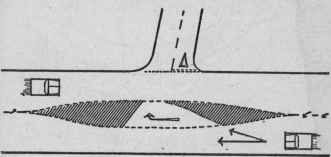

Fig. 74. "Herring Bone" lines.

They are of immense *safety* value, used correctly, and I hope will become common. Provided drivers keep off the area *except* when turning, those waiting to turn are "sheltered" from danger.

Waiting in the middle one often has a long wait while fast traffic passes on either side. Within the clearly marked "island" the right turner is removed from the grave "pile up" danger of some foolish driver overtaking (either following or oncoming) without realizing you were stationary.

DOUBLE WHITE LINES.

If you cross a line you shouldn't, you are breaking the law. If the line *continues* your side, don't ride on or cross it. You would only cross to avoid an accident or pass an obstruction or in emergency. In a crash your legal position would be bad but there is much to be said for staying alive.

Fig. 75 shows an arrangement of double lines sometimes found. Two lanes are given to traffic in one direction, only one for the other. This is usually found on long up-hill stretches to enable cars to pass slow lorries etc. Don't be lulled into thinking no one will come out of the single lane, when you are in the outer, passing lane of the two lane side. Sometimes the *single lane* has a dotted line on *its* side entitling drivers to come out if safe. Keep alert.

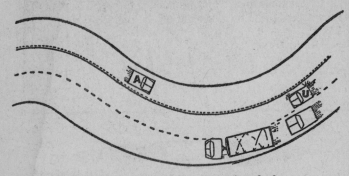

Fig. 75. A double white line with a false impression of safety.

Avoid passing at bends even in such apparently safe conditions. Others do cross these lines when unsafe and some illegally cross solid lines. You must not. *Keep awake, keep alive.*

Car U in fig. 75 would be safe only if he could see all was clear behind A.

ROAD WORKS.

Warning signs usually alert you.

If the road works block your side of the road it will be your job to *give way* to approaching traffic and, you might think, vice versa, but beware. Some people attempt to come on hoping to get away with it. It is best to stop if they do.

Traffic lights at road works normally have red or green only. Go at green, stop at red. If you are the front car to stop leave room for even a big lorry to come through or you may block everything.

FRIGHTENING THINGS THAT CAN HAPPEN AS YOU DRIVE. Burst tyres and punctures. Accelerator sticks

full on. Running out of petrol. Windscreen shatters. Engine stalls (stops). Brake failure. Breakdowns on fast roads.

BURST TYRES AND PUNCTURES.

With a puncture you get warnings, e.g. heavy steering, bumpier ride, wandering, general unbalance becoming worse. If you feel something is wrong, stop and check the tyres.

A burst (blow out) is rare. If it happens, you may hear the hiss, or, if you have hit something, expect it but possibly your warning is a sudden feeling of reduced control as the car swerves off its true line. Up to 30 m.p.h. a burst is not usually serious and even at a higher speed a *rear-wheel* burst is unlikely to cause an accident. Over 40 m.p.h. a front wheel burst may be grave. Act, never panic. If your *front* tyres are good and you *avoid* hitting kerbs or objects, you may never have one. Poor tyres and fast speeds on bad roads are likely causes.

Bursts are instantaneous. If you have one, grip the steering tightly. Use strength to try and steer past danger. Aim to slow and stop with the least possible braking to avoid further unbalancing the car. As the car swerves you may have to battle with the steering to avoid hitting anything or going over a precipice!

If the car can be allowed to slow as it loses momentum that is best but if the "burst" is not quite instantaneous you may be able to brake before the tyre is flat.

Using thin or second-hand tyres is inviting trouble.

ACCELERATOR STICKS FULL ON.

Action: *declutch* (*press it down*) *at once*. Switch off engine, into neutral and pull up as soon as possible. *If you don't panic* there is usually little danger.

RUNNING OUT OF PETROL.

This so often happens as you are passing someone using maximum acceleration. The engine splutters and fails.

Action: keep your head and stop carefully. Wise men don't drive on a nearly empty tank.

WINDSCREEN SHATTERS.

Action: stop as soon as you safely can. If need put your head out of your side window and get off the road before some idiot hits you. With modern safety screens a "clear" zone is "built in". Get your eyes near the clear part if you have glasses and you may be able to drive slowly to a garage. Otherwise it is safest to remove all glass before continuing, or fine particles may damage an eye.

ENGINE STALLS (STOPS).

Action: apply footbrake, into neutral and handbrake on. Release the footbrake and re-start engine. Act quickly and move smartly *out of danger*. As a "life-saver" if about to be hit but can't start, move on the starter in 1st gear. Get your teacher to explain.

To avoid trouble see fig. 76. It shows common causes of stalling and bear in mind the advice on page 31. Stalling is the frequent, undetected cause of many grave accidents at junctions.

Therefore whenever you are crossing lanes of traffic feed that engine.

Especially feed it at crossroads and when turning right leaving a major road if you have been waiting in the middle. Your life may *depend on not stalling*.

BRAKE FAILURE.

It's rare – but happens.

Action: Try handbrake. If it also fails due to brake-oil leak etc., don't panic and try not to hit anything. Don't lose a second. "Smash" to a lower gear, 4th to 3rd then to 2nd and to 1st, letting the engine slow you. Switch on the headlights and sound the horn continuously. With luck all should be well. Last resorts could be mounting an empty pavement and "grazing" the car side against a wall; perhaps steering, gently if possible, against a bank to reduce speed; going through a hedge into a field. Avoid the head-on killer. Miss anything, rather than hit something hard.

BREAKDOWNS ON FAST ROADS.

If you break down on a fast road, don't sit there perhaps to be hit. Try and push the car or "drive" it on the starter on to the verge if there is one. Get someone to alert traffic if any danger or put a hat or soft object on the road to

INSUFFICIENT ACCELERATION TO GIVE POWER TO MOUNT CAMBER

COLD WEATHER, FAILURE TO BOTHER TO WARM UP ENGINE PROPERLY BEFORE SETTING OFF. OR, CHOKE CONTROL LEFT OUT TOO LONG.

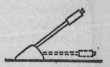

HANDBRAKE LEFT ON!

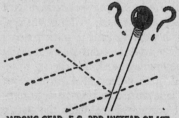

WRONG GEAR, E.G. 3RD INSTEAD OF 1ST

·GEAR SLIPS OUT; IT SHUDDERS FIRST

Fig. 76.   Common causes of stalling.

147

warn others. In France drivers have to carry a red triangle which they put on the road behind. These are valuable and can be used here, also leave the boot lid open.

SKIDS WHEN BRAKING HARD. OVER-ACCELERATION SKIDS. SIDESLIP SKIDS.
are all caused by

> (a) MECHANICAL DEFECT
> (b) ROAD CAUSE
> (c) HUMAN ERROR

or combinations thereof.

Fig. 77. Three types of skid.

SKIDS
Can skids be controlled? The nature of skids. Locked brakes. Skids when braking hard. Prevention of skids when braking hard. Correction of skids when braking hard. Over-acceleration skids. Prevention of over-acceleration skids. Correction of over-acceleration skids. Sideslip skids. Prevention of sideslip skids. Correction of sideslip skids. General advice on skids.

CAN SKIDS BE CONTROLLED?
Some motorists boast that they have 100% control of skids. Impossible, no-one has but skids are as easy to prevent as they are hard to correct.

Probably 95% of accidents blamed on skidding arise from *lack of anticipation and knowledge of skid prevention* with corresponding ignorant excessive speed. The other 5% could be genuine skids which were difficult to anticipate.

Can you get a skidding car back in control? Not easily though corrective moves may prevent a skid's severity or its worsening and enable control to be regained earlier. But there is no guarantee that *in a particular skid or its accompanying circumstances* that corrective measures will work and they often occur when there is neither time nor space to correct them.

SKIDS WHEN BRAKING HARD

Wheel(s) lock(s) up. Car slides forward, may lose sideways control or all steering may be lost. Results are accentuated if the steering is in lock (e.g. turning on a bend) or if braking on a corner or adverse camber and on downhills.

CONTRIBUTORY CAUSES

(a) MECHANICAL DEFECT
Treadless tyre(s)
Tyres soft or over-inflated, slow puncture
Front wheels (or back ones)
not having tyres of matched
tread pattern, *condition* or
type. (e.g. radial tyres mixed
with cross ply ones)
Overloaded car
Unbalanced load
Wrongly adjusted brakes
Poor suspension
Other more technical defects
causing "locking"

(b) ROAD CAUSE
Wet surface (rain)
Slippery surface (oil, etc.)
White lines (wet)
Cobbles (wet)
Loose surfaces (gravel, wet leaves
mud etc.)
Uneven surface
Downhills
"Black" (invisible) ice
or "freezing rain"
Ice/snow

(c) HUMAN ERROR
Sudden instead of progressive
braking
Excessive brake pressure by driver.
(Even with perfect brakes this can
cause wheels to lock. A
lot depends on road
conditions.)
Human Error in not making
allowances for (a) and/or (b) is the
fault that results in these skids.
BY KNOWLEDGE ANTICIPATE.
Good drivers almost never skid.
They know the terror and drive to
avoid skids.

Fig. 78. Skid when braking hard.

149

Prevention is the lifesaver and for it you need knowledge of where and why skids happen.

THE NATURE OF SKIDS.

There are three main types, those *when braking hard*, those caused by *over-acceleration* and those where the car *slides sideways* off its course (*sideslip skids*). Each of these categories can be subdivided into similar causes:

    (a) MECHANICAL DEFECT OF CAR

    (b) ROAD CAUSE

    (c) HUMAN ERROR

Fig. 77 shows this. Whichever category, a skid usually starts by a combination of (a) and (c), (b) and (c) or of all three.

LOCKED BRAKES.

Diagrammatic figures which illustrate the three types of skid (78, page 149; 80, page 156; and 81, page 159) fit into the overall picture of fig. 77. In these diagrams "locking" means when one or more wheels *stop turning*, momentum thereafter taking the car along with that (or those) wheel(s) sliding. During "locked" brake conditions there may be loss of sideways control but in explanatory text following these chart diagrams I will refer to this as such to prevent any confusion with SIDESLIP skids.

SKIDS WHEN BRAKING HARD.

Fig. 78 shows contributary causes of these skids.

PREVENTION OF SKIDS WHEN BRAKING HARD.
(a) MECHANICAL

I will clarify some of the points spotlighted on the chart, fig. 78.

Don't overload. This increases momentum (weight X speed) and alters balance making control more difficult as does lopsided loading. Take extreme care when loaded more than usual.

Always have well adjusted brakes and good tyres. Most makers recommend that brakes receive attention every 3,000 miles. Don't save pence using worn tyres.

Under inflated tyres may be detected through the steering or braking. With badly adjusted brakes or a soft tyre the car may pull to one side or wander when braking. Most dangerous. Check air at least each week.

Treadless tyres skid lethally easily.

(b) ROAD

Even on dry road you need surprising distance to stop. Study the Highway Code. Wet surfaces enormously increase the distances required. For safety follow the golden rule below.

IN WET WEATHER LEAVE TWO OR THREE TIMES THE STOPPING SPACE REQUIRED FOR DRY CONDITIONS AND REDUCE SPEEDS IN GENERAL BY ONE THIRD OR MORE.

An exercise to help you understand "locking".

You will understand fig. 78 better after experience of "locking". If you never have here is an exercise to ingrain correct reactions and illustrate the "feel" of locking wheels. It is only safe *on a wide quiet road* with *no traffic*, accompanied by an experienced driver and should be done only on a wet day. Even better is to use a specially constructed skid-pan if available.

Without exceeding 20 *m.p.h. practise emergency stops using hard braking pedal pressure.* Don't practise from faster speeds because that could be dangerous. Keep well out from the edge.

Doing these stops you should find that the car halts after sliding in a reasonably straight line. Slight loss of sideways control is allowable but any serious loss, provided the steering was straight, would probably be the result of a MECHANICAL fault and should be looked into at *once*. Sliding begins as the wheel(s) lock(s) and this critical point can be controlled with experience.

The quickest stop is one in which the wheels at no time lock, but are at all times on the point of locking and there is a *hardest pressure* on the brake pedal that achieves it. If you slide you are unlikely to be stopping as quickly.

It is difficult to know this *hardest pressure* and apply it correctly. In practice when you realise what this *hardest pressure* is (as the wheels lock), when it happens you

151

fractionally release the brake so that the wheel(s) roll again. When skidding ends you re-apply pressure as near to the *hardest pressure* as you dare. If need be you repeat this on/off process. Practise till you can do this confidently.

Here is some more about ROAD CAUSES.
Wet road surface (rain).

One reason for lowering speed generally and vastly increasing following distance in the wet is that this brake "locking" happens more and earlier. Some of the other ROAD CAUSES have a similar result. Your job is to watch and reduce speed in advance of any skid risk.

Slippery surface (grease oil etc.).

Oiliness makes roads treacherous. "Locking" can happen with the lightest of braking because the tyres are unable to grip. It is hard to detect except perhaps by a feeling of lightness in the steering. The time to be most alert is when rain begins to fall, especially after a long dry spell, because oil drops left by traffic mix with the rain and isolated patches soon spread into large areas of "ice-rink" conditions. Only after considerable heavy rain is this oiliness washed away.

Loose surface (gravel, wet leaves, mud, cow dung etc.).

Skids of all three categories (page 150) can happen on these because instead of gripping the road the tyres grip the stones or leaves etc. which themselves slide over the surface.

White lines (wet).

Many lines are painted with a cement based paint. In wet the grip on this may differ to that on the road. Avoid having to brake with a wheel on them if you can as this may unbalance braking.

Black (invisible) ice.

Difficult to detect usually being unseen but *it can be felt by a lightness in the steering* or you may discover it by an unexpected over-acceleration skid (fig. 80). In wintry conditions expect and watch for it and if in doubt stop carefully and check with your foot. Once you find it reduce speed to

15 m.p.h. or less depending how bad it is. Sometimes it appears in a form termed by weather men "freezing rain". This can be so glassy that driving may prove impossible.

Snow and Ice (including black).

If you see lorry drivers or other professionals going slowly take the hint; *snow and ice are killers*.

On snow and especially where ice forms on top of it locking can occur instantly on braking or on altering course without braking. Sometimes the best way to stop on snow is to go down the gears (no acceleration) until the car grinds to a halt in 1st. but let the clutch up cautiously each time as even a jerk can induce a skid. By this method the car is to some extent engine controlled. For normal stopping on snow or ice use gentle braking.

You may worry that the car will stick from lack of speed but this is safer than losing control. Get friends to show you how to handle a car in wintry weather before attempting it.

Road camber.

Imagine a camber like that in fig. 22 page 48 here in fig. 79. You must avoid braking hard when as far round a corner as shown in fig. 79. *Momentum* tends to carry the car straight on, not round, and braking could cause you to lose "balance" and slip on to adverse camber A, where any slide would be worsened.

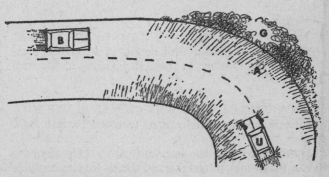

Fig. 79. Adverse camber.

To jab hard on the brakes like U has, near the limit of "balance" on the bend can result in an immediate straight on skid while the pedal is pressed. When it is realised the wheels are locked and the pedal is released to combat the skid it may be too late, the car already being in the deadly SIDESLIP type skid explained later *and thus out of control.*

Driver U in fig. 79 should have braked *harder earlier,* while on the straight or now should brake gingerly if at all so that *if* the grip of the tyres *is* strong enough he can get round without upsetting his balance. Such skids result from going too fast into the corner, *bad anticipation.*

If you do get into a SIDESLIP skid like this the car may have begun to turn but starts to slide "bodily" off the corner towards G. When this happens, but only if there is no such car as B coming near, a hard on handbrake jab may whip the back more round, enough to point the car in the direction you had hoped to go and with timed handbrake release, momentum take you there.

If skidding and a car like B, fig. 79, turned up at the wrong moment, going through the hedge at G (deliberately) might be more "Christian" than a head-on. Normally always avoid that head-on as those who miss direct hits usually survive.

The message of prevention is:

GET YOUR BRAKING DONE BEFORE REACHING CORNERS.

(c) HUMAN ERROR.

Elimination of human error comes with knowledge, experience, concentration and above all self disciplined control of speed.

CORRECTION OF SKIDS WHEN BRAKING HARD.

Correction of brake induced skids rests with three main points.

(1) Steer straight or get as straight as you can promptly. Having the steering turned causes "locking" to happen more easily and tends to throw you off course.

(2) When brakes lock release pedal pressure fractionally at once till they unlock, then at once re-apply the *hardest pressure* (discussed on page 151). If they lock again repeat this process.

(3) If the car begins to turn round you can try to straighten up by steering while the pressure is off the brake. Steer the opposite way from which the front of the car is sliding or the same way that the back is. If the back slips left, steer left and if right, right.

Sometimes however ALL STEERING CONTROL DISAPPEARS and *still does not return* after you release brake pressure although the wheels are then mechanically unlocked (raising your foot has released them). This is very frightening but a sharp hard on handbrake jab is sometimes the answer as it may induce the back wheels to start to come round. Usually once the back swings sideways steering grip returns. Instant handbrake release then allows you to steer to safety.

In extreme danger you may have to stop braking long enough to steer round and try to avoid something or someone as the safest course of action. Faced with a choice *take the least dangerous course*, e.g. bump the side of a stationary car rather than a head-on, or mount a pavement if clear.

If forced over a kerb to avoid disaster it is essential to hold the wheel strongly and steer across the kerb at a sharp not shallow angle, or you risk glancing off, back into danger. Your wheels and tyres may be ruined but with luck you will be safe.

Faced with "piling" into stopped traffic ahead with no clear pavement or other safe course open to you, because of *your own bad anticipation*, your brakes may lock with no time left for on/off re-applications. Then, to save crashing too hard into the innocent man in front, try "SMASHING" straight to 2nd and then to 1st. If time and able, hoot, to give the man time to "lock" his neck muscles which might save him neck damage.

OVER-ACCELERATION SKIDS.
Fig. 80 shows contributary causes of these.

OVER-ACCELERATION SKIDS

One or both driving wheels spin and only slightly grip or fail to grip the road to move the car. There may be loss of sideways control at the driving end as well. (Most cars have back wheel drive but some, like the Mini, have front wheel drive).

CONTRIBUTORY CAUSES

(a) MECHANICAL DEFECT
Soft or over-inflated tyre(s), slow punctures
Treadless tyre on one or both driving wheels
Overloaded or unbalanced load
Other obscure mechanical defect

(b) ROAD CAUSE
Wet surface (rain)
Slippery surface (grease, oil etc.)
White lines (wet)
Loose surfaces (gravel, wet leaves, mud etc.)
Cobbles (wet)
Black ice/ "Freezing rain"
Ice/snow
Adverse camber may accentuate loss of sideways control

(c) HUMAN ERROR
Ferocious acceleration especially in the lower gears or jerky acceleration
The above when steering round a corner or bend will make a skid more likely
Using too low a gear
Human error in not allowing for (a) and/or (b) is the main cause of these skids,
BY KNOWLEDGE ANTICIPATE
BY CAUTION PREVENT

Fig. 80.   Over-acceleration skids.

156

PREVENTION OF OVER-ACCELERATION SKIDS.

This type of skid occurs as easily when accelerating from one speed to a higher speed (e.g. 12 m.p.h. to 25 m.p.h. in 2nd) as in starting from rest. It is most serious at fast speeds and often results from harsh acceleration while cornering.

(a) MECHANICAL

Keep the car mechanically safe with special attention to the points made on the chart in fig. 80.

(b) ROAD

The best prevention is anticipation so watch for skiddy surfaces. As a learner you would be silly to accelerate so hard as to risk such a skid. On ice or grease however, it is sometimes so slippery a skid occurs with normal acceleration.

An exercise to give you experience of wheelspin.

With an experienced teacher (who may like to demonstrate first) find a gravelled drive where there is no danger. Do a standing start in 1st using fierce acceleration as you let the clutch fully up sharply. The driving wheels should spin at first but control is regained at once by dropping acceleration *without de-clutching*. The skidding ends and control returns to the steering if it was lost.

You should have plenty of room for this experiment and be ready to stop if room is limited. As it is not good for the tyres or transmission don't do it much but enough to enable you to recognize wheelspin when it happens.

(c) HUMAN ERROR

Never use harsh acceleration at corners.

Avoid accelerating ferociously on skiddy surfaces and be ready on them for wheelspin even with minimal acceleration. On snow or ice etc., wheelspin happens easily but can be minimized by at all times using the *highest* gear that will still manage to keep the car going without stalling. The secret of climbing hills in snow is to select this gear at the bottom and try not to have to change it going up.

157

CORRECTION OF OVER-ACCELERATION SKIDS.

It is important to reduce accelerating *not completely* but enough to end the wheelspin.

If the skid happens on a fast bend to stop all acceleration may turn a skid of this kind, usually the easiest to correct, into a skid of the next (SIDESLIP) type, probably the hardest. While decreasing acceleration correct the steering as necessary and as soon as control is back you can gently re-accelerate. This "sets" the car back on course.

You should thereby regain control but as you continue *think*, was it caused by my over-acceleration or by the road surface? If the latter, *slacken speed to a safe level* or you will soon be in another skid, possibly serious. Accept even a slight skid as a warning.

SIDESLIP SKIDS

Fig. 81 shows contributory causes of these.

PREVENTION OF SIDESLIP SKIDS.

(a) MECHANICAL

Don't overload and do look after your car. Give special attention to tyres, brakes, suspension and steering.

(b) ROAD

Make allowances where you know surfaces are skiddy or doubtful.

These skids are too deadly to suggest any exercise to give you experience. The only way you might get it would be on a skid-pan with a skilled instructor. But this should not be necessary. *I urge you to assimilate these instructions, anticipate dangers, employ self discipline and so avoid such serious skids.*

I will expand on some of the ROAD CAUSES.

Adverse Camber.

On poor roads camber can be bad enough to cause a skid if you meet it even slightly too fast. Such places are sometimes signed "Hazard Ahead".

Wind.

Wind can also be dangerous particularly on wet roads. It

THE DEADLY DANGEROUS SIDESLIP SKID

All the wheels, while rolling forward, drift, skidding or sliding off their steered course. *The car is completely uncontrolled.* Sometimes called 4 wheel drifting, the condition is considerably more deadly if the rear wheels are slipping away quicker than the fronts. Another skid, the front (or steering) wheel skid, is similar and the measures to be taken are in general the same. These skids generally only happen as a result of a car being cornered too fast or of hard braking on a corner.

CONTRIBUTORY CAUSES

(a) MECHANICAL DEFECT
Treadless tyre(s), slow punctures
Soft or over-inflated tyre(s)
Poor springs or faulty shock absorbers (These lessen the up and down reaction of the spring after a bump)
Front (or back) wheels not having tyres of matched tread pattern, condition or type
Different types of tyres wrongly fitted to same car.
Overload or unbalanced load

(b) ROAD CAUSE
Wet surface (rain)
Slippery surface (oil etc.)
White lines (wet)
Wind
Flood water
Loose surface (wet leaves, gravel, mud etc.)
Black ice/"freezing rain"
Ice/snow
Adverse camber alone or combined with above

(c) HUMAN ERROR
Excessive speed for conditions. (Even going straight)
Cornering too fast for conditions.
Human error in making allowances for (a) and/or (b) is the tragic fault that results in these skids
BY KNOWLEDGE ANTICIPATE
BY CAUTION PREVENT

Fig. 81. Sideslip skids.

159

normally only seriously affects a car at 50 m.p.h. or over, but a learner should not be driving that fast in rain. You usually meet it on the open road. It can hit you after passing at speed under a bridge or as you reach the end of a fir tree belt.

A gust may be powerful enough to blow a car bodily several feet, perhaps into danger. The faster you drive the more vital to keep both hands on the wheel *firmly* to maintain control if surprised. On windy days, especially in light cars, be alert.

Flood water.

To go through a flood puddle you must drop speed before reaching it depending on its depth. For deep ones it is essential to drop to a crawl while for the shallowest you generally need to slow only little. If you hit a shallow one at fair speed unawares, especially if on only one side of the car, hold the steering tight as this can throw you off course perhaps starting a skid.

(c) HUMAN ERROR.

Excessive speed *in the wet* is enough to put the car into this type of skid – *out of control*. It can happen even if you are going straight with *no other contributory cause* and is the result of aquaplaning.

Aquaplaning.

Photos 21 to 24 help explain this phenomenon only recently spotlighted in research by the Dunlop Rubber Co. Ltd. We thank them for letting us print them.

On a wet surface the traction (road grip) gradually lessens as speed rises until the wheels, instead of gripping, are skulling on a microfilm of water that builds up between the wheels and the road. As a water-skier skims over the surface at speed but when he stops sinks, so cars can "ski" and "sink' – with grip returning when they sink.

In *all types* of car this aquaplaning effect is likely to begin around 60 – 65 m.p.h. (lower if roads or tyres are not perfect). Sports cars are no more immune than others. Above this speed *the car is out of control*. With luck she may hold her course *but* the slightest bump, gust of wind, steering movement or braking could cause a skid.

Prevent such terrifying dangers by keeping speed, on wet roads, *below* 60 – 65 *m.p.h.* I have seen several cars spin off straight clear roads, their drivers presumably, unaware that they were aquaplaning and out of control till too late.

Excessive speed in other slippery conditions can have a similar result, loss of control – often unexpected. Only experience of perhaps minor over-acceleration or braking skids can warn you how fast may be safe on a particular surface.

Cornering too fast for conditions.

A moving car tends like a light beam to go in a straight line and will do so unless you bend it. A light beam you bend with a mirror (it reflects it) a car's straight on tendancy you bend by steering it. Let's call this straight on tendancy of a car its straight on momentum (weight X speed). The greater the momentum is the harder it becomes to steer the car off its straight path to where you want it to go. The steering force you can provide eventually becomes too weak to counteract this straight on momentum.

If speed is too high when a corner is reached, straight on momentum will overpower the steering force applied and the car will generally skid straight on. It will appear to slide bodily off the far side of the corner because the initial steering force applied will have first turned it partly sideways.

I have described what can happen if you go too fast.

You must, therefore, *relate speed to the corner*. The sharper it is the more you must slow *before reaching it* and even more if the camber will be adverse or the surface is doubtful.

There is a saying "Slow in, fast out" meaning that you should deliberately re-accelerate a little (or STEADILY as required) as you leave the corner, this helping to "set" the car on its new course. While the chief prevention of SIDESLIP skids at corners is the slowing beforehand this re-acceleration rule is also an important part of safe correct cornering. But do *not* over-accelerate; this could be dangerous.

Following both halves of the motto keeps the car properly

"balanced" throughout the corner and thus minimizes the SIDESLIP risk.

To be sure this balance is not upset, steering for the corner should always be gentle and progressive and you should try not to allow it to straighten itself again between movements necessitating re-steering. Equally bad is to steer too much and have to correct for it. You steer smoothly (using as many movements as needed) *enough, but not too much*.

In wet weather or if the surface is otherwise doubtful you can further refine the "Slow in, fast out" system and reduce SIDESLIP risk almost to nil. Here's how. Slow down *so much more than usual* before the corner, that you can safely begin the slight re-acceleration process *before* you start to steer round, enabling you to negotiate the whole corner on slight acceleration, increasing it as you leave, as usual. On a really slippery surface any OVER-ACCELERATION type skid that develops can be immediately counteracted by fractional release of the slight acceleration for as long as necessary.

The message is then for the wet:

Slacken speed sufficiently before the bend so that you can gently accelerate round safely.

CORRECTION OF SIDESLIP SKIDS.

These skids can turn cars round, or upside down, cause them to hit walls or jump precipices. They can happen as easily at 60 m.p.h. on wet as at 5 m.p.h. on iced-over snow.

There is no sure way of correcting once the car is gripped in a SIDESLIP skid.

Unfortunately in many serious SIDESLIP skids there is neither time or space to act except by the instinct of self-preservation – trying to steer clear of disaster and re-applying the brakes to see if they work again.

But occasionally there is room and time and various things can be tried. You can attempt to steer out of it and hope the effect will subside as the car slows naturally, neither braking or accelerating, till control returns. You can try a handbrake jab to bring the back round as described on page 154.

162

When your front wheels seem to slip away instead of taking you round a bend, and they slide off course noticeably more than the backs – a front wheel skid – straightening the steering instantly (or at least getting it nearer to straight) should be your best hope towards recovery. Most cars have built in UNDERSTEER which ensures that the fronts will always slide more easily, and earlier, under SIDESLIP conditions, than the rears. This is safer than the opposite deadly OVERSTEER characteristic which makes the rears slide first, easily putting the car into an uncontrolled spin.

But avoid last resort courses of action and remember your chief LIFESAVER is PREVENTION.

GENERAL ADVICE ON SKIDS.

Never panic. Try to get the car balanced again and back to normal. Then be ready to act as required.

Immense danger is caused by adverse road camber. This is vital to remember and allow for if you are overtaking on the "wrong" camber, normally a mad thing to do where such camber is severe. Many fast roads are "banked" (the camber is arranged to help you) but realise that even the slightest adverse camber, in skiddy conditions or sudden unforseen circumstances, is highly dangerous. At high speeds unevenness of road of $\frac{1}{2}''$ is enough to unbalance steering.

Going round a left-hand bend the camber is often adverse and your danger is skidding off your side of the road. In fig. 79 U is, positionally speaking, too far out. He should be close to his edge so that should a skid towards G happen he has the *maximum* safety margin.

In icy conditions at slow speeds in safe places, practise some deliberate minor skids which will warn you of the terror of serious ones at speed. Apart from perhaps a few slow-motion experiments with the instructor, learners should avoid snow and ice for a year or two after passing the test.

Skids usually occur on the beaten track of the snow. On untrodden snow, control can usually be regained. On a steep downhill, sometimes the only hope is to take to the edge or jump the verge as fresh snow should help you to stop.

At blind corners remember:

DO NOT DRIVE AT A SPEED FROM WHICH YOU CAN'T STOP WITHOUT SKIDDING, IN THE PREVAILING ROAD CONDITIONS, WITHIN THE DISTANCE (here limited) YOU CAN SEE IS CLEAR.

AFTER PASSING YOUR TEST, when tempted as you will be to increase your speeds, *keep all I have said in mind* – CONSTANTLY. When teaching a learner I once said at a blind corner "Slower! You might find someone lying across the road". Believe it or not, *we did*.

Finally, the Good Lord usually looks after those who never take undue risks.

FAST DRIVING
Speed. The AC Cobra. The limitations.

SPEED.

Will you become a fast driver? I don't know but I will point out several limitations and say a little about speed. It is not speed but speed in the wrong conditions that is deadly.

THE AC COBRA.

Just before the Minister of Transport brought in the 70 m.p.h. overall speed limit I had the honour of driving an AC Cobra which was then the world's fastest production car. It was put at my disposal by the generosity of the Chairman of the AC Company of Thames Ditton, Surrey.

Almost all were exported so few are seen here. To be able to drive one was not only an exhilaration but gave an impression of safety which I had never before experienced. Finger tip steering at 130 m.p.h., braking that stops you from 150 m.p.h. *in less distance than the average car stops from 70 m.p.h.*, the ability to take some large roundabouts found on trunk roads at 80 m.p.h. as smoothly as a family car at 40 m.p.h. are features worthy of comment.

Fantastic controllability *and thus safety* in this car, *entirely designed*, for speed, was the impression after a run of about 400 miles on a dry afternoon.

I honour this fabulous piece of engineering which shatters

the idea that 70 m.p.h. limits are needed for all cars. A knowledgeable minister will I hope one day make exceptions depending on make and year.

The average car, even in the hands of a skilled driver, is probably more dangerous at 60 m.p.h. than the Cobra at 140 m.p.h.

THE LIMITATIONS.

The first limitation under SPEED is the amount of effective control you have over your car. Do not expect a *family* car driven near the limit of its capacity to be as safe as a car *designed* not only for that speed but for faster.

Never be tempted to think your family car is as good as the next man's, for he may be taking chances. There are tremendous stresses and strains at speed. Fast driving is only safe in cars *worthy of speed* and this can't include some cheap or badly looked after sports cars.

Other limitations are: *self-discipline* (the most important), *speed of your reactions, ability, experience and fitness*.

Ability and experience include general skill, positioning and anticipation. Fitness includes eyesight, hearing and concentrated road-reading. It is important not to allow irritability, tiredness, illness or temporary discomfort (e.g. hunger, cold etc.), to influence driving.

It is hard to believe that we have such failings, *even in ourselves*. Human nature hates to admit to them. Reaction speeds will improve with experience; fitness you must judge for yourself.

Among the qualifications for high speeds you need to have driven several *hundred thousand* miles. It is silly to drive fast immediately after your test. May I put it more strongly? You are still a babe in knowhow. Many of your "young bloods" die because they won't accept this. Seventeen to twenty-four are the dangerous years – just the years when most cannot, on account of their age, have the mileage behind them.

For the right man in the right car, speeds above a hundred *even on our busy roads*, are as safe as the wrong man in any car at 40 m.p.h. The imperative quality at speed is self-discipline, which so few possess.

Questions. Answers.

On test you will be asked questions based on the Highway Code. Answer as fully as you can. Some of the questions that follow are the kind examiners ask; many are of a general nature included to teach you. STUDY THE CODE.

QUESTIONS.

1. Can you cross double white lines unbroken your side?
2. When must you not sound your horn?
3. Is there a general overall speed limit?
4. If someone wanted to pass when you were doing 40 m.p.h. in a 40 m.p.h. limit would you try to prevent them?
5. What do twin flashing red lights and gongs denote?
6. How do the Pelican Crossings affect drivers?
7. What is meant by a U turn and is it legal?

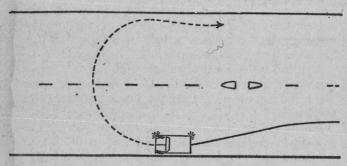

Fig. 82.   A U turn.

8. What must you do after driving through flood water?
9. What do alternately flashing red lights mean?
10. On test would you drive as fast on wet as on dry roads?
11. Are you more likely to fail for going too fast or slow?
12. What does the law make you watch for before getting out of the car?
13. Horsemen should keep to which side of the road?
14. What is a yellow "box" junction?

15. Are there ever two examiners?
16. Must you stop when signalled to do so by a policeman?
17. Can you use a left hand drive car on test?
18. If you fail to stop at a "Stop" sign will you be failed?

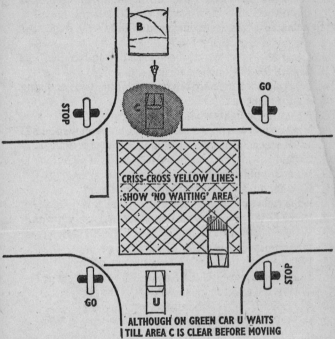

Fig. 83. A "Box" junction.

19. Why are correctly inflated good tyres essential?
20. If the driver in front signals, what do you do?
21. Where is it unwise to park?
22. If a pedestrian or motorist waves you on, would you go?
23. Can you suggest extra eye ranging for country driving?
24. What does the Highway Code advise on the subject of health?
25. Name two laws affecting ZIG-ZAG zebra crossings.
26. How should you park between two cars at the kerb?
27. Which sign denotes no overtaking?

28. Which sign means priority over approaching vehicles?
29. How should you park at night?
30. What is the shortest stopping distance given in the Highway Code from 70 m.p.h., 60 m.p.h., 30 m.p.h.?
31. What is the routine given in the Highway Code that should be followed for every manoeuvre?
32. When in a traffic queue what should you remember when you come to a zebra?
33. Describe (a) the "contra-flow bus lane" and (b) the "bus lane on road at junction ahead" signs.
34. What does a single broken line with brief gaps and long markings mean?
35. Do you go at lights when amber appears with red?
36. How should you approach and negotiate roundabouts?
37. What special action should you take when reversing?
38. Should you always use dipped headlights at night?
39. When should you dip your headlamps?
40. How should you interpret a headlamp flash?
41. What railway crossing advice is in the Highway Code?
42. Describe the change to the opposite Carriage Way sign.
43. Which sign means one lane of two or three is closed?
44. What must you do by law when parking?
45. Will the examiner watch for courtesy at all times?
46. Signs which give ORDERS are mostly of what shape?
47. What is the usual shape of WARNING signs?
48. Are DIRECTION signs always rectangular?
49. INFORMATION signs are all of one shape. What is it?
50. What Law governs the condition of your car's tyres?
51. What first aid advice does the Highway Code give?
52. What must drivers know about buses and bus lanes?
53. What rules affect loads carried or towed?
54. What special advice to other drivers is given in the Highway Code about two wheeled vehicles?
55. What extra care must you use going in or coming out of property adjacent to the road?
56. Can hazard lamps be used while driving along?
57. "If you are involved in an accident which causes damage or injury to any other person, or other vehicle, or any animal (horse, cattle, ass, mule, sheep, pig, goat or dog)

not in your vehicle, *or roadside property*" what must you do *by Law?*

58. Where should you pull up when traffic lights are red and you are the front vehicle?

59. If anything falls off your car which could be dangerous should you stop and pick it up?

ANSWERS.

1. Never, except to avoid an accident or obstruction.

2. At night, after 11.30 p.m. or before 7 a.m. in built up areas, or if stationary (unless to avoid being hit).

3. 70 m.p.h. on motorways and dual carriageways, 60 m.p.h. on all other roads except where *lower* limits are signposted.

4. No, you are not a policeman. He may be a doctor, etc.

5. A level crossing with a train due. Stop! Study the other types of warning in the Highway Code.

6. Here are the rules for drivers, in sequence:

1. Green	GO (use normal care but drivers have priority)
2. Continuous Amber	STOP (unless unsafe to do so)
3. Red (high pitched pulsating tone may tell the blind they can safely cross)	STOP! (walkers have right of way)
4. Flashing on off Amber	GIVE WAY to pedestrians still crossing (but you should go if the crossing is clear or if it clears before green comes on again)

Note that the signs facing the pedestrians show during the phases given above as follows: 1. a red man (wait), 2. still a red man (wait), 3. a green man (cross if safe) and 4. a flashing on off green man (do not start to cross – lights about to change).

7. Fig. 82. Legal except where notices ban it. Position close to kerb and when traffic is clear *in both directions* swing into full lock to get round and away in one. Leave time for a three point turn lest you misjudged the width.

8. Dry out your brakes which can lose *all* power. Drive slowly, gently holding the brakes on with the left foot (right being needed for acceleration) and driving, as it were against the brakes, till efficiency returns. *Do this at walking speed only*.

9. STOP – at level crossings, lifting bridges, airfields, fire stations, etc.

10. Not if you want to pass! Cut speed at least one-third.

11. Both are failure causes, if dangerously fast – failure.

12. That opening the door is safe; watch behind for cars and cyclists, *look over your shoulder*. Teach children this and remind passengers.

13. Horse riders keep left but sometimes the horse takes charge! Leave them extra room and pass slowly.

14. Fig. 83. Imagine a queue of traffic ahead of lorry B. You wait this side of the box even when the light is green if traffic in or beyond the box has built up and blocked your exit from it. Don't go till you see at least area C is clear. But you can move up ready, if turning right, once you can see that approaching traffic will soon clear.

15. No, but sometimes there is a supervisor to confirm that your examiner is conducting a fair test.

16. Yes, with care. It is always your responsibility.

17. Yes, you won't use hand signals but you may be asked to demonstrate them.

18. Yes, almost certainly.

19. One, because of the dangers of skidding (see page 148), two, because of the increased likelihood of a burst with worn tyres, three, because, if under-inflated, the tyre walls flex too much setting up undue heat which rapidly increases wear and may damage the walls. Damaged tyres may burst. And – it's the Law!

20. Act. Be guided by his signal – your examiner is noting.

21. Study Highway Code for complete list. Apart from specifically marked restrictions: "Always pull off the road on to a parking area if you can. You MUST NOT let your vehicle stand: on a motorway, except on the hard shoulder in an emergency; on the carriageway of any pedestrian crossing or within the area marked by zig-zag lines on either side of a Zebra crossing or in the zone

indicated by rows of studs on the approach to Pelican crossings – except to allow a pedestrian to cross; on the carriageway or verges of a "Clearway" except in an emergency; in a bus lane except to load or unload goods; on the carriageway or the verges of any section of road marked with double white lines even if one of the lines is broken, except to let passengers board or alight or to load or unload goods. Also, do not let your vehicle stand: where it would cause danger to other vehicles or pedestrians; where it would make it difficult for others to see clearly; where it would make the road narrow; where it would hold up traffic or inconvenience others; blocking the entrance to or exit from a car park; where it would prevent the use of properly parked vehicles; where emergency vehicles stop or go in and out, for example: hospital and ambulance entrances; doctors' entrances; police and fire stations; fire hydrants; entrances to coastguard stations. Never park on the road at night if it can be avoided." (See Q.29.) " ... It is particularly dangerous to park on the road in fog. Lights should always be left on in these conditions."

22. At your own risk! *Do not rely* on others' judgement.

23. Examples: Glancing momentarily down at the "lie" of the road in the valley, while you are high on a hill: anticipating the road's route by the line of telegraph poles or trees you believe are beside it. Watching out for low sports cars, sheep, etc., on hedged or sunken roads. Develop your own tricks for guessing what lies ahead.

24. "Do not a start a journey if you feel tired. Never drive after drinking alcohol or while under the influence of drugs. If you have to take drugs in the course of medical treatment consult your doctor about their possible effect on your driving ability. Do not drive if you are unwell."

25. By Law: (1) No waiting or parking inside the zig-zag-marked area on either side of the crossing. (2) No overtaking (in offside or nearside lane) on the approach side of the zig-zag area.

26. Judging if a space is long enough will come with experience. Stop beyond the space, parallel to and with

the back of your car slightly ahead of the back of the car next to the space. Aim to pull up with about 3 feet between your car and the other car. (I assume your now ingrained safety-conscience will make you check for any danger during the manoeuvre.) Reverse into the space taking almost immediate full lock to get you in. Very slowly does it. As soon as you think your front wing will clear the car in front you change back to the other lock (fully). If not in, in one go, a few forward and backward moves should straighten you up. Sometimes you may have to move partly out when safe and begin again. Practise with cardboard boxes until you never hit them. (Hitting parked cars is costly.) Photos 25 to 29 show the steps.

27. A red circle with a white background inside on which two equal sized cars appear, the left hand one in black, the right hand one in red.

28. A blue square with a thin white border, a large white arrow on the left side points up and a red arrow (smaller) on the right points down.

29. Preferably off any major road, always on the nearside *and with sidelights on* except you may park without lights provided (1) the road has a 30 m.p.h. speed limit or less, (2) you park close and parallel to the kerb, nearside next the kerb except in one way streets, (3) the car is at least 15 yards from any road junction, or (4) it is in a recognised parking place.

30. 70 m.p.h. – 315 ft., 60 m.p.h. – 240 ft., 30 m.p.h. – 75 ft.

31. "Mirror – signal – manoeuvre."

32. Leaving the crossing itself clear. Do not queue on it.

33. (a) Rectangular, with black border, blue background, picture of bus and direction arrow, reversed out in white on one half of panel, separated by vertical white line from other half, which has a white arrow inside a thin white border showing direction of normal traffic flow.

(b) Rectangular, black border, white background, picture of bus plus flow direction arrow and the words 'Bus lane' all in black.

34. Hazard; unless you can see well ahead don't cross it.

35. The Highway Code urges you not to. Nor should you go on at green until there is room for you to clear the crossing.

36. As per Highway Code with commonsense.

37. "Never reverse from a side road into a main road." Find someone to guide you if you cannot see clearly: watch for children, motor bikes, etc., *immediately* behind the car: if in doubt get out and look.

38. My advice is yes and the Highway Code states that: "You must: use headlamps at night on all roads where there is no street lighting, on roads where the street lamps are more than 200 yards apart and on roads where the street lamps are not alight; use your headlamps and rear lamps whenever daytime visibility is seriously reduced by fog, snow, smoke, heavy rain or any similar condition – to see and be seen. You should also: use headlamps at night on lighted motorways and similar high-speed roads."

39. "... When meeting other vehicles or road users, and before they dazzle the driver of a vehicle ... in front of you."

40. The Highway Code says "the flashing of headlamps has only one meaning – like sounding your horn it lets another road user know you are there. Do not flash your headlamps for any other reason." See also P. 102.

41. "Never drive 'nose to tail' over it. Never drive on to one unless you can see that the road is clear on the other side. NEVER STOP ON OR IMMEDIATELY BEYOND ANY LEVEL CROSSING." *You must study the whole of the section in the Highway Code about level crossings in addition to knowing this.*

42. A white triangle with red border containing a black pointed line which shows the direction that you will have to cross over the gap. Two black blobs indicate a gap through which the arrow is shown to pass. You read the sign from bottom to top.

43. A white triangle with a red border and black arrows showing the lanes that are clear and a slightly smaller T which is black but crossed in red showing the blocked lane.

44. You must switch off the engine and put the hand brake on. At night, leave side lights on. Obey any waiting restrictions. See page 55 and Question 29.

45. Yes, example is given in Fig. 84.

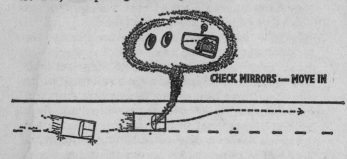

CHECK MIRRORS — MOVE IN

Fig. 84. An example of courtesy often overlooked.

46. Circular – but two vital exceptions are the octagonal STOP sign and the triangular Give Way sign. A few are rectangular – see Highway Code.

47. Triangular but a few are rectangular.

48. Normally, however some are in the shape of an arrow.

49. Rectangular.

50. Your tyres must all be suitable for your vehicle and the use you are making of it, e.g. heavy duty tyres may be required when a vehicle carries loads. You have to maintain the correct air pressures and can be in a default of the law if any tyre is worn to less than one millimetre depth of tread. More than this depth of tread must show over at least three-quarters of their width and all round. No bulges or cuts in the side walls are allowed nor are cuts of more than one inch across the tread area (or of more than 10% of the tyre width) permitted if they are deep enough to affect the body cords. Any cord showing makes a tyre illegal to use.

The wrong combination of Radial and Cross-ply tyres is illegal. The front wheels must *both* have tyres of the same type which *must not be radials* unless the back wheels also *both* have radials. The back wheels may have radials while cross-plys are on the front but I strongly advise against this. To stick to either all radials or all cross-plys is the best advice and to ensure that the front wheels have the best tyres, evenly matched for wear, is also very important. The rear tyres ought also to be evenly worn.

51. Check the Code and learn thoroughly.

52. *All drivers* should use bus lanes (but not contra-flow ones) except during their period of operation – as signposted – when: (a) beware of contra-flow permitted vehicles and or fast-moving ones sweeping along the lane especially if you have to turn or move across it, (b) no parking in a bus lane except to load or unload goods, (c) "In towns give way to buses indicating an intention to move out from bus stops if you can do so safely."

53. They must be secure.

54. "Always keep a special look out for cycles and motor-cycles, particularly when overtaking or turning. Bear in mind that two-wheelers are much less easy to see than larger vehicles and that their riders have the same rights to consideration as other road users and are more vulnerable. Drivers (especially of long vehicles or of vehicles towing trailers) should leave plenty of room for pedal cyclists in particular."

55. Check pavements: give way to pedestrians as well as road traffic.

56. No; nor should the advice be regarded as providing an excuse for stopping in a place you should not. The correct use is to warn other traffic that you are causing a temporary obstruction.

57. "If you are first on the scene of an accident you should: (a) warn other traffic by displaying a red triangle or switching on hazard warning lights or other lights or by any other means. Extinguish lighted cigarettes or other fire hazards and ask drivers to switch off their engines. (b) arrange for the police and ambulance authorities to be summoned immediately with full details of the location and casualities; on a motorway, if necessary drive on to the next emergency telephone; (c) remove casualties if in any further immediate danger but do not move them unnecessarily; give first aid; (d) get uninjured

people out of the vehicles and into a place of safety; on a motorway this should be away from the carriageway or hard shoulder or central reservation; (e) stay at the scene until emergency services arrive.

"*You must*: (a) stop; (b) give your own and the vehicle owner's name and address and the registration mark of the vehicle to anyone having reasonable grounds for requiring them; (c) if you do not give your name and address to any such person at the time, report the accident to the police as soon as reasonably practicable, and in any case within 24 hours; (d) if anyone is injured and you do not produce your certificate of insurance at the time to the police or to anyone who has with reasonable grounds required its production, report the accident to the police as soon as possible, and in any case within 24 hours, and either produce your certificate of insurance to the police when reporting the accident or ensure that it is produced within five days thereafter at any police station you select."

Sketch at the time what happened and take measurements. Get addresses of any friendly witnesses as a law case might turn on their evidence.

58. Behind the solid white "stop" line marked across the approach.

59. The Highway Code is contradictory about this; on ordinary roads it says: "Stop as soon as you can with safety and remove it from the carriageway" but for motorways "do not try to retrieve it yourself – use the roadside telephone to inform the police."

MOTORWAYS AND FAST ROADS

Learn about them. Some tips. Mirrors on the motorway. Using the right flasher. Slowing and stopping. Drowsiness. Motorway questions. Motorway answers.

LEARN ABOUT THEM.

Learners are not allowed on Motorways but here are hints for later. On test you may be asked a few "M" questions to see if you have studied the Highway Code.

176

SOME TIPS.

Beware of fog in patches, see page 133. Combat drowsiness by adequate ventilation and sufficient rest at the stopping points provided. Rests are vital to safety. Check that tyres are at the correct pressure and in good condition. A slightly higher pressure is usually recommended for motorway speeds. Confirm you will not run out of petrol.

Don't go above 60-65 m.p.h. if the road is wet. (See page 160).

Observe strict lane discipline, using mirrors and particularly never block the middle or outer lane to overtakers when you are free to move in. When yourself passing be certain it's clear behind and change lane *gradually, not sharply.* Sudden movements at speed can put the car off balance. Return to your original lane when well clear.

MIRRORS ON THE MOTORWAY.

Before changing lanes, remember some cars reach speeds above 150 m.p.h. and if you are at 60 m.p.h. they can catch you up in *almost no time.* Because a car is well behind don't assume "Oh! He's far off so I can go". It may be a fast car breaking the speed limit. Check for several hundred yards to estimate how quickly the car is catching up, then decide if you still have time.

USING THE RIGHT FLASHER.

As one can't turn right *directly* off a motorway (you have to take a slip road to the left) the use of the right winker when changing to a faster lane is good and there can be no confusion but *remember to cancel it afterwards* as on slight movements, winkers don't cancel themselves like they do on a sharp corner. The Highway Code urges you to signal for overtaking. (Right winker.)

SLOWING AND STOPPING.

After a time, the eyes and mind, focusing and concentrating far ahead for fast driving, tend to *lose all appreciation of speed.* 70 m.p.h. feels like 30 m.p.h. This is one of the most dangerous things in motoring. Allow for this danger factor and constantly remind yourself of it.

To reduce this factor's effect take frequent rests and never drive fast hour after hour. Take short walks or runs at each 20-minute rest at the stopping places provided.

The inexperienced, after miles of speed, often fail to slow early enough when they see a traffic block ahead or reach the end of the motorway. Know about this and *check on the speedometer* and slow up early. If you stop for a breakdown, illness etc. get onto the hard shoulder or you could cause a multiple pile-up; otherwise you are only allowed to stop at the rest areas provided.

If you are stopped *by* an accident ahead, keep flashing your brake lights or some ass may hit you from behind. Probably the best thing is to come to a halt well back from the trouble and go onto the hard shoulder. If your four winkers will flash simultaneously, use them as a warning.

DROWSINESS.

If you feel drowsy before a stopping centre slow and try these: open windows, pop your head in and out of the window, breathe deeply, sing, whistle, shout, shake your head, pinch yourself, slap your face, wriggle in your seat etc., but don't let these affect your driving. If still drowsy, stop on the hard shoulder to recover. If the police say they will charge you tell them not to be silly. They are sensible chaps.

MOTORWAY QUESTIONS.

1. Does the Highway Code allow reversing on motorways?
2. Can you give the main points of the Fog Code?
3. If you miss your turn off what should you do?
4. On a motorway can you overtake on the left?
5. How would you join a motorway?
6. Is there a *minimum* or *maximum* motorway speed limit?
7. Should you give flasher signals on changing lanes?
8. Do you ever *have to stop* on a motorway?
9. What do flashing amber signs beside some motorways mean?
10. Which coloured studs mean what on motorways?
11. If travelling fast on a three-lane motorway, would you drive in lane 1, 2 or 3 (numbering from left)?
12. What if I come across roadworks on a motorway?

13. What purpose do motorway amber light/panel signs have?

MOTORWAY ANSWERS.

1. "You must not reverse or turn in the road, or cross the central reserve, or drive against the traffic."
2. "Slow down; keep a safe distance. You should always be able to pull up within your range of vision. Don't hang on to someone else's tail lights; it gives a false sense of security. Watch your speed; you may be going much faster than you think. Do not speed up to get away from a vehicle which is too close behind you. Remember that if you are driving a heavy vehicle it may take longer to pull up than the vehicle ahead. Warning signals are there to help and protect; observe them. See and be seen —you must use your headlamps or fog lamps, and rear lamps. Use your windscreen wipers. Check and clean windscreens, lights, reflectors and windows whenever you can. If you must drive in fog, allow more time for your journey." The Ministry also advises heavy lorries to stay in the left lane while all other vehicles move out of it.
3. Keep going to the next exit slip road; you are not allowed to turn or reverse back.
4. Never, ever! Unless traffic is queueing outside you.
5. Wait for a long, repeat long, gap in the nearside lane traffic and time your acceleration in the slip-road so that you join the nearside Motorway lane by "merging" into the gap. On a busy day, you may have to stop a while, *well before the slip road end*, till a gap materializes.
6. No minimum but it's unwise to go below 40 m.p.h. even in the nearside lane owing to the high general speeds on Motorways. The maximum is 70 m.p.h.
7. Yes, essential if traffic behind. Give way to faster over-takers. Signal in ample time and *cancel afterwards*.
8. Only in emergency or if required to by police, emergency traffic signs or a flashing red light above your lane.
9. Danger – you must drop to 30 m.p.h. or less when the lights are flashing until you are sure it is safe.
10. Amber mark the right-hand carriageway edge and red

the left edge; green studs separate the slip roads from the motorway itself.

11. If empty 1, if 1 is full 2, and for passing only 3.
12. *Slow up* and be prepared for single lane conditions.
13. They are for your safety – danger may exist although you cannot yet see why. "In dangerous conditions, amber lights flash and a panel in the middle of the signal shows either a special temporary maximum speed or which lanes are closed. When the danger has been passed the panel of the next signal will show (without flashing lights) the end of restriction signal. On most motorways, the signals are on the central reserve at intervals of not more than two miles and they apply to all lanes. On some very busy motorways, the signals are overhead, one applying to each lane."

THE TEST

The car. You. Driving there. Announce your arrival. Before leaving home. How long is it? The examiner. Author's message.

THE CAR.

Be sure your car is in good order and properly "tuned", is not cold and runs sweetly. Check that the handbrake will hold the car on the steepest hill, that the brakes are correctly adjusted and the tyres are in good condition and at the right pressures. Fill with petrol, clean all the windows and check all lights and flashers.

If there is thick fog or ice, or snow, your test will normally be postponed. Phone the test centre and confirm in such weather.

YOU.

Are you dressed warmly if it is a cold day? We react better when warm. Remember the window will have to be open, for giving hand signals. You need not worry about the examiner being cold as he knows and dresses accordingly. If the test is in the morning don't go to it on an empty stomach after no breakfast.

DRIVING THERE.

Ask your teacher to let you drive to the test centre, or if it is a long distance drive the last few miles. This gives on the day "in the groove" confidence. Arrive in good time but not "hours" early.

ANNOUNCE YOUR ARRIVAL.

Announce your arrival, as, if there has been a cancellation you may be able to go straight away. Take your driving licence, glasses if worn, insurance certificate and appointment notice to the test centre with you.

BEFORE LEAVING HOME.

Refresh your memory on the signs you have *already* studied before leaving for the test. You can amuse yourself while waiting at the centre by giving them a final run through. Don't worry if you seem to have last-minute forgetfulness. You are unlikely to fail for wrongly answering one or two questions.

HOW LONG IS IT?

The test lasts about three-quarters of an hour. It may seem long but don't worry, the examiner may be waiting for certain traffic situations to arise to see how you cope. A long test won't necessarily mean failure, nor will a short one. Note: safety belts can be worn if desired but are not yet insisted upon, however, the Highway Code urges their use at all times.

THE EXAMINER.

The examiner may not talk much, some do, some don't. Like all people some are quieter than others. If yours seems quiet or bored for example, don't feel he is against you; it is almost certainly no more than a quirk of personality.

AUTHOR'S MESSAGE.

I hope you have battled through this far and *done your homework*. I have *done my best for you*. In this book are results of years of research and the experience of over one million miles driving without an accident claim. Many thousands of pounds have been risked to enable you to buy the book for the cost of a few cigarettes.

Please therefore follow its messages.

Any who would like help with problems arising during learning that are not explained or who have criticisms may write to me care of the publisher and I will do my best to help. Please enclose a stamped addressed envelope.

GOOD LUCK AND DRIVE JUST AS CAREFULLY AFTER YOU PASS – ALWAYS.

INDEX

A

A.C. Cobra, 164
Accelerator, 20, 52
Accelerator sticks on, 145
Accidents, 64, 101
Ahead arrow, 116
Air, 151
Ambulances, 75, 170
Animals, 65, 70, 170
Anticipation, 67, 70, 72, 74, 95, 107, 154
Aquaplaning, 160
Arrows on the road, 116
Arrows, green filter, 118
Automatic transmission, 20, 137

B

Beacons, 73
"Black" ice, 149
Blind bends, 66
Blind spots, 100
Brake lights, 68
Brake pads, 25
Brakes, adjustment, 68
Brakes, disc, 25, 107
Brakes, failure, 54, 146
Brakes in reverse, 42
Brakes, "locking", 38, 60, 150
Braking, 36, 37
Breakdowns, 146
Bridle path, 32, 65

Burst tyres, 145

C

Camber, 47, 87, 153, 163
Car parks, 45
Carelessness, 65
"Cats' Eyes", 66
Certificate of Insurance, 167, 178
Children, 65, 70, 78, 81
Choke, 32
Cloudbursts, 133
Clutch, biting point, 22, 34, 39, 54
Clutch plates, 20, 22, 35
Clutch "slip", 23, 35, 45
Clutch, use, 18, 19, 36, 39, 40, 41
Cobbles, 149, 156
Common sense, 14, 47, 53, 67, 73, 75, 90, 99
Concentration, 57, 70, 109
Congestion, 118
Conscience, 132
Countryman, 65
Courtesy, 79, 82, 109, 119
Cows, 65
Cross signs, 115
Crossing in front, 119
Cul-de-sac, 46
Cutting corners, 65, 66
Cyclists, 19, 68, 70, 77, 81, 89, 118

D

Daily Limit, 42, 56
Day-dreaming, 110
Dazzle, 135
Declutching, 33
Defensive driving, 84
Dipped beam, 134
Disabled driver, 172
Dodgem cars, 30
Doors, 56
Double white lines, 70, 143
Downhill starts, 54
Drink, 100
Driving shaft, 20
Drowsiness, 175, 177
Dual Carriageways, 66, 110

E

Emergency stop, 37, 38, 60, 73, 74
Engine braking, 41
Examiners, 56, 74, 100, 122, 167, 168
Excessive speed, 159, 160
Experience, 56, 63
Eye switching, 58, 70, 87
Eye training, 70, 73
Eyesight, 165

F

Fast driving, 164
Filter arrows, 118
Fire Engines, 75
Fishy eyes, 43, 50
Flints, 62
Flood water, 159
Fog, 132
Fog, in patches, 133

Foglamp, 132
Foot-brake, 19, 25, 36
Freewheeling, 54
Freezing rain, 149
Friction, 39

G

Gateways, 65
Gears, 19, 21
Gears, changing, 39, 40
Gears, cogs, 22
Gears, speeds, 39
Gears, steering column, 22, 23
Gears, use of, 54, 55
Glasses, 100
Golden rules, 63, 70, 92, 109, 132, 151, 164, 171
Gravel, 149
Greasy roads, 140, 152, 157
Gum Boots, 36

H

Hairpin bend, 65
Hand signals, 33, 61, 69, 102
Hand signals, left hand, 104
Hand signals, right hand, 103
Hand signals, slowing down, 104, 105
Hand signals, to police, 104
Handbrake, 19, 25, 26, 87, 89, 94, 139
Hazards, 69, 74, 92, 158
Headlights, 132
Headlights, Dipswitch, 134

Headlights, Driving, 134
Headlights, Flashing, 102
"Head-Ons", 84, 122
Heart-of-Safety, 70
Heavy steering, 145, 151
Hedges, 100
Herring bone lines, 143
High beam, 134
High heels, 18
Hill start, 13, 27
Homework, 14, 51, 56
Hooting, 66, 72, 78, 81
Horn, 19, 65, 166
Horn push, 72
Hump back bridges, 79
Hypnotism, 136

I

Ice, 152, 157
Ignition switch, 31
Indicators, 19, 77, 102, 126, 175
Indicators, at roundabouts, 127
Innocent, 74
Instinct, 38
Insurance, 14, 122

J

Jay-Walker, 72
Jerky starts, 26
Judgement, 57, 73, 81, 87

K

Kerb, 47, 55
Kerb, distance from, 62
Kickdown, 139

L

"Labouring", 69, 114
Lane discipline, 78, 127, 176
Lane positioning, 116
Law, 143
Leap-Frogging, 68
Left hand drive, 168
Level crossing, 170
Lever, 23
Licence, 14
Life Saver, 36, 110, 163
Light Shooter, 120
Light steering, 152
L-Plates, 14, 72, 116

M

Madmen, 74
Maniacs, 120
Manoeuvring, 42, 138
Mental Preparation, 114, 123
Merging, 122
Mile-an-hour, 39, 48
Mini-Bikes, 43
Ministry of Transport, 125, 164
Mirror adjustment, 18, 19
Mirror, "blind" areas, 18, 59
Mirror, extra, 57
Mirror, use, 58, 59, 94, 123
Mist, 132
Momentum, 68, 161
Motor bikes, 59, 70, 90, 97, 99
Motorways, 175
Mud, 152
Muscles, 19

185

N

Narrow Lanes, 64
Nerves, 14
Neutral, 22, 30, 36, 93, 94
"No-Claims" bonus, 92
Nose-to-tail driving, 67

O

Obstructions, 75
One Way Street, 121
Open Practice, 13, 26
Open Space, 13, 27, 36
Over-Acceleration Skids, 156
Over Confidence, 42
Overloaded Car, 149, 150, 156, 159
Overtakers, 62, 82
Overtaking, 79

P

Panic, 129, 133
Parking, 35, 166, 169, 173
Parking on a Hill, 55
Passing, 81
Pedestrians, 70, 73, 74, 78, 100, 109, 112
Petrol runs out, 145, 174
Petrol Tank, 20
Pile-ups, 67, 74, 133, 143, 155
Pinking, 69
Pivot, 17, 34, 35
Police, 75, 103, 121, 176
Police signals, 121
Positioning, 57, 76, 89, 91, 95, 107
Pulling Power, 19, 21
Punctures, 145

Q

Queue, 67, 101
Questions, 14, 166

R

R.P.M., 21
Radial Ply Tyres, 149
Rain, 69, 133
Ratchet, 25
Reverse Gear, 22
Reverse, into side road, 13, 45, 50
Reversing, 42
Reversing, at night, 137
Right-of-Way, 73, 75, 79, 82, 85, 89, 99, 102, 129
Road Reading, 72
Road Works, 144
Roundabouts, 124
Roundabouts, round the block, 128
Runaway cars, 55
Running Commentary, 56

S

Safety Way, 14
Safety Belts, 107, 108
Scenery, 70
Seat Adjusting, 18
Selector Lever, 137
Self Centering, 28
Self Discipline, 136, 158, 165
Shock Absorbers, 159
Side Lights, 132
Signals, slow down, 74
Signs, Give Way, 85, 94, 95
Signs, Halt, 85, 87, 94
Signs, No Entry, 117

Signs, No left turn, 117
Signs, No right turn, 117
Signs, Slow Major Road
   Ahead, 85
Signs, Stop, 85, 87, 94, 96
Skid, Control, 148
Skid, Correction, 148, 154,
   158, 162
Skid, Prevention, 148
Skid, When braking hard,
   149
Skidding, 38, 148
Slip Roads, 91
"Slow-in-fast-Out, 161
Smooth Start, 30
Snow, 149, 153, 157, 163
Soapbox Carts, 65
Speed, 64, 72, 100, 164
Speed Limits, 63, 176
Spotlight, 137
Spray, 133
Stalling, 31, 36, 87, 88, 97,
   146
Steep Opening, 66
Steering damage, 48
Steering, grip, 28
Steering, hand position, 17,
   27
Steering, heavy, 145, 151
Steering, light, 152
Steering, one hand, 30
Steering wheel, 17, 27
Stopping distance, 68
Street lighting, 136

T
T Junction, 85
Teachers, 14, 57
Temper, 57

Tenseness, 57
Test, Application for, 14
The Test, 45, 120, 179
Thinking Time, 67
Three Lane Roads, 82
Three Point Turn, 13, 35,
   45, 46
Tick over, 21, 22
Time lag, 67
Top, 39
Torrential Rain, 133
Traffic, 46, 51, 52
Traffic lights, 78, 112
Traffic wardens, 121
Twilight, 134
Two Way Roads, 62
Tyres, 48, 62
Tyres, burst, 145
Tyres, damaged, 48
Tyres, soft, 156, 159
Tyres, thin, 145

U
Unbalanced Car, 149, 156,
   159
Unmarked Crossroads, 101
Unusual Customs, 120
Uphill Start, 52, 139
U-Turn, 166

V
Vans, 43, 67, 81, 130
Ventilation, 169

W
Wet, 69, 70
Wet leaves, 149

Wet nights, 120
Wheelspin, 157
Wide One-Ways, 122
Willpower, 132, 136
Wind, 158
Windscreen, shatters, 146
Windscreen, steamed up,
  132
Windscreen washer, 134
Wintery Conditions, 152

Wipers, 19, 132, 133

Y

Yellow "boxes", 167

Z

Zebras, 68, 73, 74, 78,
  109

NOTICE

While this book is strictly copyright the publishers are pleased to allow a short extract of not exceeding one page to be quoted without prior permission from them, *provided* acknowledgement is given in the following terms.

"From LEARNING TO DRIVE IN PICTURES, by A. Tom Topper, a paperfront, published by Elliot Right Way Books, Kingswood, Surrey, U.K."

Here, written simply and with skill, is the book for you. Its purpose is to calm your nerves and remove your fears, by giving hundreds of sample questions and answers. It is arranged so that the many parts of an answer to a particular question, that may be drawn from different parts of the Highway Code, are given together.

Hundreds of drawings, some reproduced with permission from the Highway Code, are included to make learning as easy as is possible for you.

Uniform with this book

* * *

THE MOTORCYCLE DOCTOR

by John Robinson

This manual assumes no prior knowledge on the part of the reader. It has been planned with straightforward step-by-step language to cover all the popular machines available around the world.

With special emphasis on diagnostic trouble-shooting, John Robinson leads the owner/rider through every aspect of tender loving care and breakdown solving he or she is ever likely to need.

You are sure to save £££'s and £££'s as you grasp the basics of how bikes work and how to keep your own machine running like a bird.

Few could be better qualified to write this than John Robinson, for many years a technical expert to the magazine Motor Cycle Mechanics.

Uniform with this book

CAR DRIVING IN TWO WEEKS

by L. Nathan, R.A.C. Diploma

***What the Critics say:

Daily Telegraph – "Immensely practical"
Daily Sketch – 'Excellent for new motorists'
The Motor – 'A book worth having'
The Autocar – 'No learner could fail to benefit'
Birmingham Evening Post – 'Certainly the best'
Edinburgh Evening News – 'A notable contribution'
Highland News – 'A bible for "L" drivers'

Millions have been enabled to pass their test with *Car Driving in Two Weeks.*

Uniform with this book

* * *

THE CAR DOCTOR A-Z

by B. C. Macdonald

Symptoms - Causes - Cures

UNIQUE!

This book is an astonishing A.B.C. faultfinder. Look up the symptoms and the book tells you the causes and cures. Precise step-by-step details of the action to take in every circumstance, routine or emergency.

No driver should be without this book.

You can save £££s in garage fees.

Behind the book stands our GUARANTEE:
Return for full money refund if you disagree this is the
world's greatest book on the subject.

*   *   *

Many readers will want to secure the same author's com-
panion volume, CAR REPAIRS PROPERLY EXPLAIN-
ED. This covers maintenance and explanations of how a car
works and used alongside "The Car Doctor" will be of enormous help to the reader.

Both Uniform with this book

BLMC MINI REPAIRS

by B. C. Macdonald

Here the author of the best-seller "THE CAR DOCTOR",
now applies all his knowledge and experience to the Mini.

He has evolved an entirely new formula in the writing and
layout to make it easy for YOU to understand. All the
chapters are written on the same basic plan, i.e.,

Section 1: General data

Section 2: Fault Symptoms

Section 3: Causes and cures. Written with the analytical
step-by-step approach which has made B. C.
Macdonald famous.

Section 4: and additional sections: special procedures for
more complicated repairs and servicing, maintenance, etc.

Uniform with this book

ELLIOT RIGHT WAY BOOKS
KINGSWOOD, SURREY, U.K.